Louis B. Freiman

FREEING THE HUMAN SPIRIT

"Dr. Louis Fierman is a very experienced psychiatric clinician and esteemed teacher. *Freeing the Human Spirit* reflects his style and values and emphasizes honesty, straightforward communication, perseverance, and humor. The vignettes in the book bring these values to life by combining a discerning clinical eye with a direct and vivid prose."

—Malcolm Bowers, Jr., M.D.,
Professor of Psychiatry, Yale University

"Lou Fierman is a rare bird in the jungle of psychiatry: He actually listens to his patients—and he has meaningful conversations with them, too! Why is this so rare today? Because psychiatrists are taught to study brains and neuro-transmitters at the expense of understanding persons and the existential reasons for their behaviors. Dr. Fierman's candor frees the human spirit, and the conversations documented here could give disillusioned psychiatrists a new sense of purpose and meaning in their work. I recommend it."

—Jeffrey A. Schaler, Ph.D., author of
Addiction Is a Choice

Also by Louis B. Fierman, M.D.

Effective Psychotherapy:
The Contribution of Hellmuth Kaiser

The Therapist Is the Therapy: Effective Psychotherapy II

FREEING THE HUMAN SPIRIT

A Psychiatrist's Journal

LOUIS B. FIERMAN, M.D.

Blue Dolphin

Published by Blue Dolphin Publishing, Inc.
P.O. Box 8, Nevada City, CA 95959
Orders: 1-800-643-0765
Web: www.bluedolphinpublishing.com

ISBN: 1-57733-100-1

Library of Congress Cataloging-in-Publication Data

Fierman, Louis B.
    Freeing the human spirit : a psychiatrist's journal /
Louis B. Fierman.
        p. cm
    Includes bibliographical references and index.
    ISBN 1-57733-100-1
        1. Psychotherapy—Case studies. 2. Psychiatry—Case
studies. I. Title.

RC465 .F493 2001
616.89'14—dc21

                                                    2001037876

Printed in the United States of America

10   9   8   7   6   5   4   3   2   1

Dedicated
To the memory of my dear brother,
William "Bill" Fierman

CONTENTS

ACKNOWLEDGMENTS

Hellmuth Kaiser taught me that psychotherapists need not regard their work as work but rather, in a sense, as play; an enjoyable encounter with a fellow human being. This is not to ignore or shirk the therapist's full responsibility for the conduct and outcome of psychotherapy, but rather to emphasize the quality of spontaneity, openness and sharing that characterizes the communicative-intimacy offered by the therapist to the patient in effective psychotherapy.

The stories in this book exemplify the joy and drama as well as the therapeutic power of achieving a communicative-intimacy relationship with a patient. My primary acknowledgment for this book and for my being a psychotherapist goes to Hellmuth Kaiser.

A close second goes to my wife, Ella Yensen, Ph.D., an experienced, practicing psychotherapist who has collaborated with me and scrupulously reviewed the entire manuscript. Her consultations, advice and critiques have permeated all the stories and their commentaries in this book. Her keen sensitivity to the subtleties of behavior has enriched my understanding and portrayal of all the therapeutic encounters described. Her support and encouragement were the driving forces that led to the completion of this book.

My friends, the late Leo H. Berman, M.D., a distinguished Connecticut psychiatrist; Jerry Krakowski, a student of the work of Hellmuth Kaiser; and John M. Rakusin, Ph.D., a prominent New Haven psychotherapist, now retired, have all read parts of the manuscript and offered generous and useful critiques. Dorothy Carr and Howard P. Kahn, Ph.D., also listened to drafts of some of the stories and offered valuable consultation.

Ellen McDermott, Office Manager of Psychotherapy Associates, provided her technical expertise and constant encouragement. The staff of Blue Dolphin Publishing, under the direction of Paul Clemens, were also most helpful and supportive in preparing the text for publication.

PREFACE
The Magic Power of Communicative Intimacy

I believe it is close to the truth that most "schools" of psychotherapy and psychoanalysis rely on interpretive and pedagogic activity as the principal therapeutic effort. These "insight" oriented therapies have the common denominator of a structured relationship in which it is tacitly agreed between patient and therapist that, in a sense, the patient suffers directly or indirectly from a lack of knowledge about himself; or, to be more precise, about that part of himself which is suppressed, repressed, preconscious or unconscious.

A second premise is that the therapist has superior, expert or esoteric knowledge, is more familiar with this part of the patient than the patient is himself; and that, finally, if the therapist can successfully impart this knowledge to the patient and also assist him by imparting additional relevant knowledge, the patient will use this information to cope with and integrate these heretofore hidden aspects of himself and become healthier and happier.

It is my belief that any clinician working within the insight framework of psychotherapy sooner or later becomes dissatisfied and disillusioned with these premises. After exhausting the many rationalizations available to account for treatment failures, the psychotherapist arrives at a turning point in which these basic issues are themselves at stake. Many prominent therapists have promoted therapies that deviated either partially or completely from the Freudian analytic, insight-oriented approach. As an alternative they focus on the relationship between therapist and patient rather than on the history of pathogenesis.

Hellmuth Kaiser was such a therapist. Trained in orthodox Freudian psychoanalysis, he was subsequently influenced by his teacher, Wilhelm Reich. It was Reich who advocated that the analyst should delay formal psychoanalysis with his patients until he had first confronted and attended to their attitudinal resistances by dealing directly with the patient's overt and communicative behavior. Reich called this phase of therapy "character analysis" (Reich, 1949).

Kaiser, however, went beyond Reich's admonition to delay formal psychoanalysis temporarily. He gradually came to the realization that therapy was more effective if, instead of reverting back to orthodox analysis as Reich had taught, he would continue throughout the therapy to engage the patient in a here-and-now, interactive, nondirective, communicative-intimacy relationship. Kaiser described his gradual evolution to this final stance vis-a-vis his patients in a monograph written in third person: *The Universal Symptom of the Psychoneuroses: a Search for the Conditions of Effective Psychotherapy* (Kaiser, 1965a).

Kaiserian psychotherapy offers an alternative therapeutic approach which when applied by his followers has had promising results and has encouraged them to pursue his attempt to develop and formulate a somewhat new theory and practice of psychotherapy. In attempting to define and describe this method, it soon becomes apparent that there is a subtlety and complexity about it that precludes its reduction to a few simple formulations. Its illusiveness has to do with a delineation of the therapist-patient relationship.

Kaiser's writings on his innovative psychotherapy have been published and discussed in two previous books (Fierman, 1965 and 1997). However, it is best described and understood in the context of actual clinical transactions between therapist and patient such as has been presented in this book. It is easier to begin by saying what it is not rather than what it is. That is, the therapist disavows explicit pedagogy, interpretation, confrontation or strategic maneuvers as therapeutic activity.

The Kaiserian method incorporates a position by the therapist whereby the patient is regarded as being literally free to do in the therapy hour whatever he pleases. The only limitations are those determined by the therapist's personal needs and interests, such as time, financial arrangements, self-protection, etc. Beyond the therapist's personal limitations, the situation and the relationship are left essentially free and unstructured and the therapist's activity becomes simply sharing with the patient those of his reactions to the patient's behavior that he deems appropriate.

Basic to the orientation of the therapist in this therapy is the clinical phenomenon characterized by Kaiser as the "Universal Symptom." This symptom is no more nor less than the duplicity in communication manifested by psychologically disordered people (Kaiser, 1965a, p. 36-37). When patients present themselves in psychotherapeutic treatment, the Kaiserian therapist is uniquely positioned to detect and reflect on their duplicity. Kaiser's orientation equates "genuine" and "direct" communication with psychological health and the Universal Symptom with psychological disorder. This orientation plus the sensitivity of the therapist to the Universal Symptom determines the therapist's focus of attention on the patient's pattern of duplicitous communication and his own experience or reaction to it.

However, Kaiser advocated that the therapist should not try directly to change the communicative behavior of the patient. He regarded dependency as the core psychopathology of neurosis, and the Universal Symptom of duplicity in communication represented the effort of people to establish "fusion relationships" in order to avoid the dread of feeling existentially alone and separate. Thus, Kaiser designed his therapy as being nondirective to avoid reinforcing the basic dependency of the patient.

Cure of the patient was to be obtained by the therapist offering the patient a relationship which I have come to call "communicative-intimacy" (Fierman, 1997). The basic assumption of Kaiserian therapy is that consistent "genuine" behavior and communication on the part of the therapist is all that is necessary and sufficient to effect a cure. The commitment by the therapist to "communicative-intimacy" as being the potent ingredient of effective psychotherapy precludes any directive efforts or maneuvers and makes the therapy nondirective. The only "rules" are that the patient be physically present with an intact central nervous system, and that the therapist not withdraw psychologically from his patient.

The relationship offered by the therapist consists solely of "communicative-intimacy" and his activity consists of freely responding behaviorally and verbally to the patient's verbal and nonverbal behavior. His conviction is that the patient's neurosis will eventually give way to the power that a communicative-intimacy relationship with the therapist will have on him. The therapist's responses more often than not will take the form of observations and comments about the patient's Universal Symptom; namely, the patient's duplicity in communication. However, the intent of the therapist is not to confront the patient, but rather, to share with the patient the therapist's impressions and reactions to his behavior (Fierman, 1997).

Similar to Kaiser, Dr. Peter Lomas, a prominent British psychoanalyst, also abandoned psychoanalytic orthodoxy, and instead advocated a "personal psychotherapy." In his book, *The Case for a Personal Psychotherapy* (Lomas, 1981), he described what he thought a therapist should not do: "The therapist should not, in a polite or conventional way, smooth over difficulties or (worse) humour the patient or adopt a patronizing bedside manner; nor should he be committed to an opposite dogma— a relentless pursuit of the truth at all costs on all occasions, with an accompanying need to open up old wounds in the interests of theoretical rigor; his primary aim should not be to understand the patient, nor to learn from him, nor to enlarge the frontiers of science through his studies of him, nor to assuage his own loneliness or to seek a substitute for child, spouse, parent or lover. He should not use the patient to treat, vicariously, his own neurosis or as a captive audience for his own particular brand of theory. . . . The perspective I am here proposing for psychotherapy is . . . embarrassingly unspecific . . . it refers to a situation in which one person is aiming to help another to grow by offering him a relationship that has much in common with those in ordinary living but takes place in an unusual context" (Lomas, 1981, p. 43-44).

In a later book (Lomas, 1999, p. 91) he also urged spontaneity and genuineness as crucial qualities for psychotherapists' responses to their patients: ". . . I have used the term 'spontaneity' to indicate a quality of response that comes–insofar as this is possible–from the core of one's being rather than behavior that has been rehearsed according to a plan, strategy, or theory. It seems likely that, being unrestrained, the spontaneous mode of being would be less of an effort. The difference is akin to that between a formal dinner party in which one feels the need to behave in an acceptable way and meeting an old friend with whom one can leave one's pretenses behind. Such a meeting is not a scientific search for truth but, in some ways, there is more likely to be truth around."

Lomas disavowed analytic interpretation: "Explanation and interpretation are means by which we may attempt to control and diminish the full force of being." (Lomas, 1987, p. 4). In addition he advocated "intimacy" rather than "insight" as a goal of therapy: ". . . the most apparent impairment (in patients) is an inability to make sufficiently close and realistic relationships with others. It is primarily for this reason that people consult psychotherapists . . . a major task of the therapist is to help his patients towards a greater capacity for intimacy" (Ibid, p. 69).

It is of interest that these two psychoanalysts, Lomas and Kaiser, both independently arrived at such similar views and innovations about psychotherapy. Many other therapists have also shifted from a psychoanalytic, insight-therapy perspective to an interactive, communicative-intimacy, nondirective approach. The following selection of quotes are illustrative of this trend.

Victor E. Frankl (1973, p. 24f.): "...one can aptly speak of human meeting *(Begegnung)* as the actual agent in the modes of acting in psychoanalytic treatment. The so-called transference is also probably only a vehicle of such human meeting. ... *Within the framework of psychotherapy, the methodology and technique applied at any given time is least effective of all: rather it is the human relationship between physician and patient which is determining.*"

Erich Fromm (1962): "Instead of being an observer, I had to become a participant; to be engaged with the patient; from center to center, rather than from periphery to periphery."

Virginia Satir (1987, p. 23): "I have learned that when I am fully present with the patient or family, I can move therapeutically with much greater ease."

Harry Stack Sullivan's "therapeutic technique focused on the interaction between the therapist (conceptualized as a *participant-observer*) and the patient within the therapy setting" (Cushman, 1992, p. 46).

Irvin D. Yalom (1980, p. 410): "The relationship is the therapy." "When technique is made paramount, everything is lost because the essence of the authentic relationship is that one does not manipulate but turns towards another with one's whole being."

The question remains: how and why does a sustained experience of a patient with a therapist engaging him in a sharing, nondirective, communicative-intimacy relationship have a healing and transforming effect on the patient's psychopathology and behavior pathology. While neither Martin Buber nor Carl Rogers used the term "communicative-intimacy" in their writings they both advocated the healing and therapeutic effects of just such a relationship.

Martin Buber, the renowned Israeli philosopher, wrote on the nature of man in his seminal thesis, *I and Thou* (Buber, 1923). In it he maintained that only in an "I and Thou" relationship with other humans could a person realize, experience and confirm his full authentic reality as a person. In such a relationship the persons involved would relate to each other in an open, communicative and sharing, nonjudgmental and accepting, genuine and authentic, nonauthoritarian and egalitarian manner. Buber further advocated that experiencing such a relationship had a psychological healing or psychotherapeutic effect on one or both the parties. Buber characterized this effect as "healing in the meeting" and wrote (1952): "The technical superiority of the therapist is not required, but rather his or her actual self." He stated later (1960), "The patient experiences the therapist's authenticity and is empowered to give up the inauthentic aspects of his own character and personality which are manifested through the patient's symptoms and character pathology."

A nondirective psychotherapy based on Buber's "I and Thou" relationship has been developed and described as "Dialogical Psychotherapy" by Maurice S. Friedman. He wrote (1985, p. xi): "All therapy relies to a greater or lesser extent on the meeting between therapist and client. . . . But only a few theories have singled out the meeting—the sphere of the 'between'—as the central, as opposed to the ancillary, source of healing." He goes on to state (Ibid. p. 3), "What is crucial is not the skill of the therapist, but rather what takes place *between* the therapist and the client."

Nondirectiveness has also become the *sine qua non* of Rogerian psychotherapy. In a review of the history of the development of nondirective therapy (Raskin, 1948), Carl Rogers is credited with replacing the directiveness of Freud, Otto Rank and other insight-oriented psychoanalytic psychotherapists with "nondirective acceptance." Rogers also advocated that therapists offer their patients (Rogers preferred the term "clients" rather than "patients") unconditional positive regard and a full, open, sharing, empathic and congruent relationship. He stated, "I had come to recognize quite fully that the therapist must be present as a person in the relationship if therapy is to take place" (Evans, 1975, p. 25). Later Rogers wrote (1980, p. 129), "I find that when I am closest to my inner intuitive self . . . whatever I do seems to be full of healing . . . simply my *presence* is releasing and helpful to the other."

I believe that the following basic principles of psychotherapy provide a rationale for the proposition that a communicative-intimacy relationship offered by a therapist can be in itself an effective psychotherapy:

1. Psychotherapy is conceptualized and defined as the providing of a psychotherapeutic *experience* by a psychotherapist for a psychologically disordered patient.

Now the reader may ask what purpose is served by formulating such a principle. It seems rather circular, stilted and supererogatory. After all, are not all therapies clinical experiences? The answer is that this emphasis on experience is made in order to distinguish this therapy formulation from other therapies and other formulations about therapy which emphasize or equate psychotherapy

with the goals, techniques or activity of the therapist
(i.e., supportive therapy, behavior therapy, uncovering
therapy, insight therapy, character analysis, interpretive
therapy, etc.), or with the goals, responses or activity of
the patient, as implied in such often heard characteriza-
tions as "the patient is not 'really' in therapy," or "the
patient resists his therapy," or "the patient does not want
to change or be helped," etc.

This principle is made to establish a contextual point
of view in regard to psychotherapy in which, although one
may characterize a therapy as emphasizing patient activity, therapist activity, transactions or interactions, the
therapy remains, nevertheless, experiential and something more than the sum of its observable component
behavioral parts. Moreover, this principle defines psychotherapy as an experience provided for the patient by the
therapist. The definition thus places responsibility
squarely on the therapist and does not call upon the
patient to do anything in, for or to his therapy other than
to be present (Kaiser 1955). Psychotherapy as thus defined does not include any rules or conditions for the
patient which he can either obey and submit or disobey
and resist. In short, the patient's psychotherapy is what
happens to him when he is with his therapist.

**2. The psychotherapeutic experience provided by the
therapist is the *therapist-patient* relationship sustained
over a period of time long enough to overcome, dissipate
and make unnecessary the patient's psychological illness.**

This principle is an elaboration of Principle #1. It
equates the therapeutic experience with the therapist-
patient relationship and defines the proper "dose" of the
"medicine" as being "enough" to "cure" the patient. Both
Principles #1 and #2 invite an empirical as well as a

contextual point of view. Changes which hopefully occur
in the patient in therapy are viewed as reactive consequences of the relationship experience rather than as
direct results of goal-directed, technique-oriented activity
by the therapist.

**3. The structure or nature of the characterization of
the therapist-patient relationship is determined by the
position or role and the activity of the therapist.**

This principle will be elaborated by succeeding principles which will characterize the position and activity of
the therapist. In itself, however, it reiterates the proposition that it is the therapist and his activity which makes
this relationship therapeutic and not the patient and his
activity. It also suggests as a corollary that this relationship is unique and different from other kinds of relationships. This uniqueness is derived specifically from the
position and activity of the therapist.

**4. The activity of the psychotherapist is determined by
his position or role which, in turn, is determined by his
orientation in regard to mental illness, mental health and
psychotherapy.**

This and succeeding principles suggest that there is an
alternative to the goal-directed, insight-oriented, technique-oriented activity which characterizes most psychotherapies currently in practice. These therapies require
that the therapist's behavior must in some specific way be
directed toward achieving some specific goal or some
specific response or some specific effect in the patient.
What is frequently overlooked is that this activity stems
from an assumed position or role of the therapist with the
patient, and that this position is determined by the
therapist's orientation and not by the clinical needs of the
patient. For example, if the therapist equates the patient's

illness with his suffering from the effects of repression or suppression of painful thoughts, affects, memories or motives, and if he believes that to achieve insight into this state of affairs will cure him, then the therapist will assume the position of an investigator or teacher or promoter of insight, and his activity will be accordingly probing, uncovering, pedagogic, interpreting or clarifying. Similarly, if the therapist equates the patient's illness with being uninformed and, therefore, unable to make sensible decisions, and if he believes the patient will be relieved of his illness by receiving good instruction and advice, the therapist will assume the position or role of the patient's advisor and his activity will be directive.

The therapy I am describing does not have an orientation of being goal-directed or technique-oriented. The only "goal" of this therapy, if it can be called a goal, is to establish and promote a communicative-intimacy relationship between the patient and the therapist. The only "technique," if it can be called a technique, is to relate to the patient in a nondirective, genuine, sharing way.

5. The Kaiserian psychotherapist equates mental illness with the patient's disordered communication.

The communication disorder, which Kaiser has called "duplicity," is manifested in therapy by all patients in their speech as being incongruent, indirect, ungenuine or unintegrated. It is the means by which the patient attempts to relate to and engage the therapist on a verbal as well as nonverbal level of implicitness, covertness and indirectness. It is the means by which all patients deal more or less with their basic dependency and their existential "angst" by seeking what Kaiser has identified as fusion relationships with others, including their therapists. It is the means by which all patients more or less try to deny their existential separateness from others and try to create an illusion of fusion with others. This principle asserts the ubiquity and universality of this phenomenon among psychologically disordered people of whatever diagnostic category. Kaiser has termed this manifestation the Universal Symptom. It can be observed to some degree in patients in therapy and, indeed, the psychotherapeutic situation, particularly the patient-therapist relationship, seems to bring it out and intensify it.

This principle does not take issue with or contradict any known theory of behavior, psychological functioning or symptom or character formation. It only asserts a phenomenological fact as far as patient behavior in therapy is concerned, and for purposes of therapy makes this phenomenon central to the patient's illness.

6. The psychotherapist's orientation in regard to mental health equates psychological health in the patient in therapy with lessening or disappearance of the patient's communication disorder.

In successful therapy the patient's communication becomes less duplicitous or even disorder-free and he becomes able to relate to and engage the therapist consistently on a level of explicitness, directness and genuineness. These changes are accompanied by all the other manifestations of a successful result in psychotherapy, i.e., symptom alleviation, maturation, self-sufficiency, improved relationships, social adjustment and enhanced creativity.

It should be mentioned here that cure in psychotherapy is always a relative matter, and that no one is ever consistently or completely non-neurotic. Similarly, the disappearance of the patient's communication disorder is also a relative matter and is never achieved 100 per cent.

Nevertheless, the therapist's orientation in regard to psychological health in therapy is in terms of the hypothetical ideal state.

7. The psychotherapist's orientation in regard to psychotherapy is that psychological health in the patient can best be promoted by the therapist devoting himself exclusively to relating to and engaging his patient on a level of nondirective explicitness, directness and genuineness.

This principle maintains that if a psychotherapist devotes himself exclusively to responding behaviorally and verbally in a genuine, spontaneous, nondirective, explicit and straightforward manner to his patient's behavioral patterns of communicating and relating, then the patient's psychological disorder will eventually give way to the impact of his therapist's genuine responses. This principle thus defines the therapist's position or role and his activity which make the therapist-patient relationship unique and therapeutic. The therapist's sole and exclusive desire, intent and purpose with the patient is to engage in genuine dialogue.

The therapist's responses may often take the form of observations and comments about the patient's disordered communications. However, even this activity is not goal-directed. It is not confrontation in order to get the patient to change, but rather, it is to share with the patient the therapist's empathic impressions and reactions. The exclusive single-purpose concern of the therapist in relating genuinely to his patient makes the relationship egalitarian, and precludes the deliberate use of advice, rule setting, directing, pedagogic interpretations and confrontations or other authoritative or authoritarian maneuvers, since they do not serve the therapist's sole interest in actively engaging his patient in mutually genuine communication. Whatever rules or limits are introduced into the therapy situation by the therapist are done so because of the therapist's personal needs, i.e., time, money, self-protection, responsibility to the community, etc., and are recognized by the therapist as being necessary for him but irrelevant for the therapy of his patient. Beyond such personal limitations the therapy situation and the relationship are left free and unstructured by the therapist as he devotes himself exclusively to receiving and reacting to his patient's behavior.

This principal asserts that given enough time and frequency of contact between therapist and patient, the patient will find help and clinical cure as a result of his relationship with the therapist who is devoted solely and exclusively to overcoming the obstacles the patient puts in the way of maintaining genuine and intimate dialogue. This is the main principal of this therapy and the only one that empirically and directly provides the motivational or intentional basis for the therapist's position and activity. However, it should be emphasized that all the principals formulated above only provide a rationale for psychotherapeutic activity, and as such may gratify the need that therapists seem to have for a rationale for their psychotherapeutic activity.

But a rationale for psychotherapeutic activity is not meant to be part of the psychotherapeutic activity itself. The only requirements for a therapist to engage in psychotherapeutic activity with a patient are that he has a patient and that he knows how to engage in psychotherapeutic activity. In this activity his theories, principles and rationale are quite unnecessary. It may even be harmful to therapy if the therapist combines his psychotherapeutic activity with concern for conforming or confirming his theories or principles of illness and therapy. It would be harmful to the extent that it detracts and distracts the therapist from being receptive and sensitive to the actual phenomena of the therapy and responding genuinely, spontaneously and effectively to his patient's behavior.

INTRODUCTION
Case Vignettes

"But just what is it that you do?"

That question has been asked of me many times when I have lectured or appeared on panels at meetings concerned with psychotherapy. Despite my efforts to describe in great detail the nondirective, communicative-intimacy activity by those who practice "Kaiserian," existential, interpersonal therapy, the questioners usually feel incompletely answered until descriptions of actual therapies including verbatim interchanges between therapist and patient become available as demonstration.

A few examples of such verbatim interactions can be found in my previous books: *Effective Psychotherapy: The Contribution of Hellmuth Kaiser* (New York: Free Press/ Macmillan, 1965) and *The Therapist Is The Therapy: Effective Psychotherapy II* (Northvale, NJ: Jason Aronson, 1997). For those readers interested in reading more about what can happen in successful encounters between a therapist and his patients, I present these stories. They are all true stories, most with happy endings. This is by no means meant to imply that I have not had my share of unsuccessful cases, but I can attest that most of my patients have benefitted from their therapy; of course, some more than others. To protect the confidentiality of the patients described in these stories all identifying facts or circumstances have been altered.

A final word about "freeing the human spirit." All humans are endowed with the potential to become persons who are free of neurotic or psychotic symptoms, free to adjust peacefully to the constraints and laws of their community, free to engage in intimate and loving interdependent relationships, free to cope competently with "the slings and arrows of outrageous fortune" and free to seek fulfillment of their God-given talents, aptitudes and creativity. But, unfortunately, for many, perhaps most people, such freedoms will not be realized unless the individual can find and experience sustained interpersonal relationships with other people that will promote, enable and support the development and achievement of such freedoms. This is critically essential for all persons in order to reach their full potential. Parents, siblings, families, friends, teachers, spouses, lovers and psychotherapists may be providers of such relationships, but for many, no such relationships are available and their lives remain stunted. Only a relatively few humans ever reach and enjoy their full potential to become free spirits.

For me, the promise of effective psychotherapy enabling people to reach their full potential was the attraction that compelled me to become a psychiatrist specializing in psychotherapy. And, the secret reward, known to all serious and ambitious psychotherapists, is that doing psychotherapy is in itself an enabling experience for therapists themselves and helps them to reach and enjoy their own potential.

1

YOU'RE NOT TOO FAT—YOU'RE TOO SHORT

Kathy told me she weighed about 200 pounds and had tried every known diet plan with the same dismal results . . . first a period of rapid weight loss followed by a gradual return to overeating and excessive weight gain. "I've had it, Doctor," she broke out as she wept, "if this therapy doesn't work I'll kill myself!"

I regarded her silently as she wept. She was about five-feet-five, long brunette hair, neatly dressed, modest make-up. It occurred to me that even though overweight, she was still very attractive. "Kathy," I said as I handed her my box of tissues, "it's hard to believe you seriously regard obesity as a capital crime or a sin deserving of the death penalty."

She did not respond but continued to weep silently. After a long pause I continued, "Fortunately, psycho-therapy is supposed to help people with problems such as

yours and I'll be glad to work with you as much as I can."
She dried her eyes and we then arranged for a weekly
psychotherapy.

She used her initial hours to present an unsolicited
biography. *(Kaiserian psychotherapy is nondirective and
precludes the therapist taking a formal history or conduct-
ing a formal mental status examination. Rather it allows
the patient's history to emerge as part of the patient's
undirected spontaneity. This patient behaved as if she was
quite willing to comply with her assumption, probably
based on her preconceptions about therapy, that she was
supposed to present her chronological life history.)*

She was the only child of a surgeon father and an artist
mother, both retired and living in San Diego. She was 32
years old and claimed normal weight until her marriage
ten years ago. She had one child, now a five-year-old
healthy girl. Kathy taught art in a local high school where
her husband, Ted, also taught history.

"Ted refuses to have anything more to do with me
because of my weight," she sobbed, "and my father is so
disgusted he finally ordered me to go into therapy and
even agreed to pay for it."

"Your father is usually not generous with you?"

"Well, the problem is he hates my husband," she
explained, "He's never forgiven me for marrying Ted, who
was a college classmate of mine. It's because Ted's a
Liberal and Father regards all Liberals as Communists.
He refused to send us any money even though we were
broke. He even wrote me out of his will; but at least he set
up a trust for my daughter. I visit my parents every
Christmas with my daughter but without Ted."

As the weeks of therapy passed I increasingly became
aware of Kathy's child-like demeanor. For instance,
whenever she spoke about relatives in her life, she would

refer to them only by their first names without explaining who they were. "Kathy," I finally commented, "I notice that you keep referring to your family and relatives by their first names as if I should know who they are; as if I, too, were a member of your family."

She blushed and then responded, "I guess I do feel you have become a member of my family. You are sort of fatherly—like the father I never had." And then rather coquettishly she added, "But you haven't said a word about my losing weight. I'm down ten pounds and seem to have no trouble sticking to my new diet."

"Congratulations. I never doubted that you could control your weight once you set your mind to do it."

"But why haven't you ever tried to figure out why I overeat or why I started gaining weight in the first place. Aren't you interested and isn't that what you're supposed to do?"

"'Yes' to the first question and 'No' to the second."

"Well, I'll tell you what I think anyway," she said, smiling and cheerful. Over the next several sessions she reported her childhood memories of being in guilt-ridden competition with her mother for the attention and affection of her father. Her mother was obese and her father would cruelly confront her mother's obesity with Kathy's adolescent slim figure. He would also compare her mother's mediocre academic history with Kathy's superior scholastic record. Worst of all, he was scornful of her mother's unsuccessful efforts to achieve recognition as an artist compared to young Kathy's precocious talent as a creative artist. Kathy blamed herself for contributing to her mother's chronic depression over her father's abusive behavior and his obvious preference for his daughter's presence and achievements. Kathy finally escaped from the family triangle by going off to a distant college and then getting married despite her father's disapproval. However, her father's abuse of her mother continued and as her mother's depression worsened, Kathy's guilt increased as did her overeating and weight.

"Well, Doctor, what do you think of my self-analysis?" Kathy asked.

"How would you want me to think of it?"

After a long pause she slowly said, "I want you to think that I'm the most interesting and attractive patient you've ever had, especially since I've lost another ten pounds." I was taken aback and silently pondered her provocative statement. She became flustered and embarrassed and suddenly began weeping profusely as she had done in her first hour.

The hour was nearing its end and after several more minutes of painful silence I decided to try and lift her apparent despair and said flippantly, "You are the most interesting and attractive patient I have ever had." She stopped crying instantly, stared at me a few moments and then we both broke out laughing as the hour ended.

Christmas was approaching and as she left for her annual visit to her parents in San Diego, eager to display her svelte figure to her father, she assured me she would continue her therapy on her return. Two weeks later she reappeared and to my surprise began her hour by once again weeping profusely. I waited patiently until she finally began to explain between wracking sobs, "My father says that now that I've lost all my weight I don't need therapy . . . and he refuses to pay for it any more . . . and you know we don't have any insurance . . . so if you will take an I.O.U. until my husband and I get a raise at the school, I promise we will pay you back. . . . I know if you stop seeing me now I will gain back all the weight I lost!"

"Kathy," I said slowly and deliberately, "you want to substitute me for your father and have me subsidize your diet and your therapy instead of your father. I'm afraid that would seriously compromise your therapy for me to do that. I am not your father or your substitute father. I'm sure you and your husband can find a way to continue to pay for your treatment each month as you have in the past." She shook her head in disbelief, exclaiming, "I never thought you would be so mercenary and heartless!" and then she left abruptly.

I was relieved to see her show up for her regularly scheduled appointment the following week. Angry and petulant she reported that she and her husband had both found after-school jobs to supplement their meager school salaries and also pay for her therapy. "I hope you're satisfied now," she complained bitterly. In the following weeks she filled her hours with recriminations, accusing me of being uncaring, mercenary, duplicitous, worse than her father, etc., etc. And to my dismay she rapidly began regaining her lost weight. Each hour she appeared looking markedly heavier than she had the previous week.

"I keep worrying about money and can't stop bingeing and I'm getting terribly fat again and it's all your fault!" she said tearfully, "How can you do this to me? Don't you care at all about me and my weight?"

Finally, in desperation, I reacted, "Kathy, of course I'm concerned about your welfare, but, frankly, I'm not concerned about your weight. You're an attractive, healthy, active woman in spite of being somewhat over-weight. Actually, as far as I'm concerned, you're not too fat—you're too short! You should be going to Height Watchers instead of Weight Watchers." Instantly her wailing stopped and suddenly she threw her box of tissues at me. I dodged the box as she said scornfully, "Is that supposed to be funny? Did you take a course in jokes in medical school? You have a warped sense of humor."

"Maybe so, Kathy, but perhaps you have a warped sense of tragedy," I countered. The next few weeks saw her gradually becoming less angry and more confident as she successfully returned to her dieting and began to lose the weight she had so rapidly regained. Finally, once again svelte and cheerful, she reported that she had become reconciled by phone with her father, had succeeded in getting him to accept her husband as a non-Communist son-in-law, and even persuaded her mother to return to the painting hobby she had abandoned years before.

At her final hour she brought me a gift—an abstract painting of hers, consisting of large splotches of pink and brown colors. "Can you tell me what is this supposed to represent?" I asked.

"That's a painting of my former fat body lying on my living room couch," she explained and departed after a farewell hug. To my knowledge there has been no recurrence of depression or obesity.

* * * * *

This patient reflected dynamics inherent in the triangulation of her parents with herself. As an only child she had no siblings to dilute her parents' intense focus on her, and the parents' conflictual relationship was played out in their interaction with her. Kathy became involved in their conflict over her mother's obesity and she was compelled to deal with her father's unabashed use of her in his conflict with her mother.

While she allegedly was in competition with her mother for her father's affection, she also had followed her mother's career choice as an artist and clearly identified with her, even gaining weight like her. Although her comments focused on her father and his judgments, her behavior suggests strong identification with her mother. Her struggle with obesity apparently was in part learned from her parents and their conflict around her mother's weight.

She married a husband knowing her father disapproved of him and, in her therapy, she identified me as a father substitute "like the father (she) never had." It is apparent she wanted to escape behavior patterns established in her nuclear family and was willing to persist in her therapy even after her father withdrew his support. My indifference to her weight helped her to break away from her family's obsessive attention to it.

Sometimes humor can be an effective way for therapists to make a point. I did not learn this in medical school as she claimed, but discovered its usefulness in doing therapy. Humor with this patient served to break through her self-pity, aroused her anger and motivated her determination to control her own life and relationships in constructive ways. The painting she gave me in farewell symbolically left her "former fat body" with me while she went on to a new life.

Treating eating disorders in both children and adults is fraught with uncertainty with a high risk of relapse and recidivism. There are multiple causative factors but stress seems to be ubiquitous. Effective psychotherapy can reduce stress and eventually overcome the patient's need to comfort as well as harm one's self through bingeing.

2

I'M AL, NOT ALEXIS

Alexis loved cars. He would buy abandoned, broken-down, wrecked antiques, have them towed to his back yard and spend his free time repairing, refinishing, re-painting and restoring them to their former function and glory. He would drive them around his suburban town for a few days or weeks and then sell them, usually for a handsome profit. Unfortunately, his joyful hobby did not fit well in his marriage and his wife of three years finally divorced him, claiming that the inordinate amount of time he spent working on his cars left her neglected and frustrated. One year later his personal physician referred him to me for psychotherapy because of his complaints of depression and insomnia.

"Doctor," he began, "there's something wrong with me. It's been over a year now since my wife divorced me and I'm still having dreams about her and thinking about her and missing her all the time."

Alexis de Laval was thirty-eight, robust, trim build, conservatively dressed with starched white shirt, tweed jacket and tie, looking puzzled and uncomfortable. After several minutes of silence I commented, "It's hard to tell from your statement whether you are more concerned with the loss of your wife or with your falling behind some sort of imagined time schedule for normal mourning."

"What? Imagined? You don't think its abnormal for me to keep missing her even though its been over a year since the divorce?"

"You seem to believe that there are established schedules and standards of normalcy and abnormalcy for people reacting to painful loss and it seems hard for you to give up that notion."

He laughed as he explained, "Well, you see, I'm an engineer, a mechanical engineer from M.I.T., and I guess I'm used to things being quantified and measurable. Anyway, does that mean I don't need therapy after all, since you say I'm normal?"

"I don't think I said that, but, in a way, psychotherapy can be regarded as a cure for "normalcy", for people who live lives of constriction by always adhering to alleged rules of correctness and normalcy and who never risk crossing those arbitrary boundaries. They've lost their spontaneity, creativity and passion and their happiness is constrained by their scrupulosity. Psychotherapy is supposed to free the human spirit."

Alexis had listened intently and then said solemnly, "I don't know if you're aware of it, Doctor, but that description fits me to a T. I think I'd like to try your psychotherapy." We arranged to meet weekly.

In the weeks that followed, Alexis painted a word picture of an unhappy, lonely childhood. He was the only child of a wealthy New York art dealer of French royal descent whose frequent world-wide travels rarely permitted him to be home long enough to have a meaningful relationship with his son. Alexis was raised by his mother and her servants. She had christened him Count Alexis de Laval but he called himself Al Laval after he left his home to attend prep school and college, followed by two years of submarine duty in the Navy.

His mother was an active socialite, hosting lavish parties which her little son had to attend, hair curled and dressed in little Lord Fauntleroy garb. He reported that she also made him sit with her for hours listening to recordings of classical music in order to make sure he appreciated Bach, Brahms and Beethoven. What it did, in fact, was create an aversion to the classics, and as an adult he would listen only to country music.

He met his wife, a young pretty artist, at one of his mother's society parties. They had a brief courtship, married and moved to a small town in southern Connecticut. He bought into a car dealership and, when not selling expensive sports cars, he pursued his hobby of restoring antique cars.

"I guess I was a bad husband and neglected my wife shamefully, but I loved her and she should have given me another chance. Also, I should have made more of a fuss over her affair with our neighbor."

"Alexis," I said, "you frequently refer to things and people in your life as if you have reason to believe that I know who and what you're talking about."

Alexis looked chagrined and responded, "I guess I do feel as if you've known me for a long time and sort of know all about me without my having to tell you the details. Crazy, no?"

"No—maybe just a way of feeling less alone and isolated in the world." *(Hellmuth Kaiser [1965a] has described the ubiquitous behavior of neurotic patients in seeking "fusion relationships" with others, including their therapists.)*

Alexis conceded that his childhood had been lonely. He felt smothered by his pretentious mother and recalled how he fantasized an imaginary playmate as he played with his toys.

"Well," he finally said, "to get back to the story of my wife's affair; one day I noticed her purse lying open on the table in our bathroom and inside I could see her diaphragm. When I asked her 'how come?' she flew into a rage, telling me that since I was having 'affairs' with my cars and neglecting her sexually she had been forced to seduce our bachelor neighbor in order to satisfy her sexual needs. I told her that I understood and was sorry and would always be available for her whenever she desired sex. This only infuriated her more. She called me 'schizoid' for not being angry and jealous about her affair. She also accused me of being 'gay' for not seeking more frequent sex with her even though we did have sex every week or so. That's when she started divorce proceedings. Was she right, Doc? Am I gay without knowing it?"

"No, but you do tell your stories in a flat, unemotional way. I suspect your feelings about your unhappy marriage must be rather intense but they seem blocked within you. I suspect you rarely, if ever, cry about the painful experiences you've had both in your childhood as well as in your adult life."

Alexis was silent, but after several minutes took some tissues and began silently crying. He wept for several minutes, then blew his nose, dried his eyes and as he left the office he said, "You're right, Doc. To my memory that was the first cry I've ever had."

Over the next several weeks there appeared to be a gradual unfreezing of Alexis' stiff and formal bearing. He became more cheerful, more talkative with more jokes and laughter. References to his ex-wife and former marriage gradually disappeared.

His married business partner introduced him to an attractive single friend and Alexis began a serious courtship of this woman. He brought detailed, lively accounts of his new and old life experiences to the therapy. It was clear his depression had lifted, his obsessional mourning for his ex-wife was over and there had been a breakthrough of his affect block.

Despite his improved state there was no hint from him about terminating his therapy. It was as if he were content to continue indefinitely to come week after week eager to report on his current activities, experiences and creative ideas. Finally, a session began with his saying, "Doc, I'd like your advice about an idea I've been working on. You know I had submarine duty during my Navy career. I now live near a nuclear submarine base. Well, I've been thinking how easy it would be for me to steal a nuclear submarine! I could go to a used Army-Navy clothing store and buy an old Admiral's uniform. Then I would rent a limousine to drive me to the submarine base. I would get out of the limo, pay the driver, march up to the submarine dock, salute the Navy guard and announce, 'I'm Admiral Alexis de Laval and we're taking off!' No sailor would dare challenge an Admiral and I'm sure the crew would simply follow whatever orders I gave them and we'd sail that sub right out of the harbor into open sea. However, my only problem with the whole idea is figuring out what in the

world would I do with the sub after I stole it! Any suggestions, Doc?" He was obviously bursting with gleeful pride
over his outlandish but creative fantasy.

"Alexis, that fantasy is a metaphor for your current life
situation. You've cast off your obsessional depressive con-
strictions of your true self and have become a cheerful,
creative free spirit, but you don't seem to know what you
want to do with your new-found freedom. I suggest you
look into your heart of hearts and confront your talents
and interests and commit yourself to pursuing them,
particularly if they offer promise of improving the quality
of people's lives." *(Advice giving is not consistent with
Kaiserian nondirective psychotherapy, but spontaneity and
genuineness are essential aspects of the communicative-
intimacy relationship, and in this instance I was moved to
respond to the patient's aimlessness.)*

For the next few weeks Alexis did review his varied
interests, searching for an avocation that would satisfy his
urge to be committed to a meaningful life purpose and
goal. Finally he reported, "You know, Doc, for a long
while I've been toying with the idea of starting a mail-
order business for people who are having trouble finding
rare and unusual tools that would help them with their
crafts and hobbies and projects. I frequently have that
problem myself and have to search all over to find the
precise tool I need."

In his subsequent sessions he reported with increasing
enthusiasm his evolving plan to start a new rare tools
mail-order business. He finally leased a warehouse to
store his supply of rare tools, but his business plans soon
involved moving to another state.

"Let's plan on this being my last hour with you," he
stated one day. "Let me hear from you," I said as we shook

hands warmly and parted. Months later he wrote that his new business was flourishing; that he had married the woman he had been dating and that he had legally changed his name from Count Alexis de Laval to simply Al Laval.

* * * * *

This therapy was about freeing the spirit of this patient from the constraints imposed upon his spontaneity, creativity and emotional expression by a constricted and unhappy childhood, including a neglectful father and a pretentious and overly controlling mother. Parental neglect and domination can be more hurtful to a child's spirit and psychological well-being than physical abuse. His history of choosing country music and rejecting classical music advocated by his domineering mother is an example of pseudo-independent behavior commonly observed in adolescents. The adolescent often needs to know first what his parents want of him before he can know what it is that *he* does *not* want himself.

This weekly therapy lasted about eighteen months but seemed to be successful in altering his obsessive-compulsive character structure. His sharing with me his fantasy of stealing a submarine revealed his increasing release from neurotic constriction and movement toward becoming a free spirit. His growing dependency on the therapist and the therapy was aborted by my direct confrontation of his aimlessness. There was little need for further intervention since the patient intuitively used the therapy situation himself to allow his own creativity, individuality and independence to emerge.

3

STRIPTEASE

Nancy Barnes appeared promptly for her first appointment. She strode resolutely into the office and without hesitation elected to recline on the office couch rather than use the lounge chair opposite mine. She was in her early thirties, attractive, short and slim, brunette hair, bright make-up, pearl earrings and necklace, diamond wedding ring, wearing a colorful flowered summer dress. There was a long pause. She fixed me with a piercing gaze and, watching my every move, slowly took a pack of cigarettes out of her small beaded purse. Virginia Slims.

"Is it O.K. with you if I smoke?" she said.

"It's O.K. with me," I replied as I handed her an ashtray, "but I doubt that it's O.K. for you." She smiled and slowly lit her cigarette with her pearl Bic lighter.

"I guess you're right," she said, "I should stop someday." Still staring at me, she began to smoke slowly and silently. Finally she stated, "I want to be perfectly frank with you, Doctor Fierman. I wanted to go to Doctor Jackson with my problem but he told me his schedule was full and gave me your name instead. I wanted Doctor Jackson because he helped a friend of mine who had a similar problem."

Still staring she again lapsed into silence. After several minutes I decided to break the silence and said, "You keep staring at me as if you were looking at Egyptian hieroglyphics and trying to figure out their meaning."

She laughed and explained, "No. It's only that I'm embarrassed by my problem and don't know quite how to begin." Taking a deep breath she went on to describe her "problem." She reported that her husband, aged 45, had survived a severe heart attack the previous year but still suffered from recurrent chest pains and had been warned to avoid stress at all costs. However, he continued to work full time as an accountant and was at his office, away from home, five days a week. Meanwhile, Nancy had fallen in love with her husband's best friend, an insurance agent, aged 40, a divorced bachelor. They had been engaged in a passionate affair for the past three months. He frequently would come to her suburban house where they would have sexual intercourse.

Nancy claimed that she constantly worried that her husband might come home unexpectedly or otherwise find out about her affair and that the shock would kill him. Her dilemma was that she wanted to continue her romance with her lover but also felt she should end the affair in order to relieve her guilt and fear about possibly causing her husband's death.

Nancy began to weep as she described her impasse and I tried to console her by offering assurances that psychotherapy was supposed to help people resolve such dilemmas. We agreed to meet once a week.

As the weeks went by she proved to be a punctual patient, always arriving on time, always electing to lie on the office couch, always beginning by staring at me with fixed gaze and using her hours to review her childhood and adolescence, meeting her husband at college, marriage at age 21, several miscarriages and her decision not to seek employment but to do volunteer work at a local hospital.

Meanwhile, her affair continued unabated although her expressions of guilt and fear became less frequent and less intense. However, I gradually became aware that at successive weekly hours she seemed to be wearing less and less clothing! First her dresses became replaced by skirts and blouses; then the full skirts were replaced by miniskirts and then by walking shorts; the blouses by sleeveless tops to be replaced in turn by halters; the walking shorts by short shorts; and, finally, one hot summer day she arrived wearing a fur coat which she casually discarded to reveal herself clad only in a bikini!

"I hope you don't mind my bathing suit," she said as she draped herself on my couch. "It's so hot these days that's all I wear all day at home," and then she resumed her monologue pattern of blandly reviewing her life history.

But, of course I did mind since I found her voluptuous exhibitionism extremely arousing and distracting. I tried hard to avoid looking at her seductive pose, particularly since she was, as usual, watching me closely. I listened in agitated silence while she droned on and on about her childhood. Finally, at the end of the session, I was able to state with some trepidation, "Nancy, you are a beautiful woman and you have a beautiful body, and although I'm an old man, I'm not *that* old! So if you want me to pay full attention to what you have to say to me when you are here, I suggest you stop this slow striptease that you have been performing these past several weeks!"

Nancy became flustered, silently gathered up her fur coat and left without a word. The next session she arrived modestly dressed in her summer dress, sat in a chair rather than the couch and announced primly, "This will be my last session here, Doctor Fierman. Do you remember that I told you I wanted to see Doctor Jackson but his schedule was full and so he referred me to you? Well, at that time I also asked him to let me know when he had an opening, and he has finally called me and I'm going to continue with him starting next week!" All this said with the fixed stare that so characterized her behavior throughout her six weeks of therapy.

I gulped, took a deep breath and speaking slowly and deliberately as I usually do when saying confrontational things that might upset my patients, I said, "Of course, Nancy, you are free to choose any therapist you want, but you know perfectly well that you could have simply phoned to cancel your therapy with me. I assume you came today instead of calling because you wanted to see how I would react to your announcement, just as you wanted to see how I would react to your wearing less clothing, and, possibly, just as you have some desire to see how your husband would react to finding out about your affair with his friend!"

"Doctor Fierman! How can you think such a thing! I would never do anything like that just to see how you would react! It would have been mean for me to just stop seeing you without coming in to explain why." She became tearful and the hour ended after I wished her well with her therapy with Doctor Jackson.

A few weeks later I met Jackson at a psychiatrists' meeting and inquired as to how Nancy's therapy was doing. Doctor Jackson was an elderly, paternalistic, eclectic psychiatrist not affiliated with any particular school or brand of psychotherapy. "Lou!" he exclaimed, "I've been meaning to call you about her. How could you have let her go on and on with that awful affair with her husband's best friend! Didn't you realize it could kill him if he ever found out!"

I was dumbfounded at this reproachful outburst. "Well," I retorted defensively, "Just what did *you* do about it?"

"Why I simply insisted that she had to stop seeing that man or else it would lead to her husband's death!"

"And she did?"

"Of course! I wouldn't have allowed her to do otherwise!"

"And you're still seeing her?"

"Of course not. There's no need now that she's stopped the affair." We parted and I staggered off amazed at this account of a directive psychotherapy conducted by a dogmatic, domineering doctor with a passive, submissive, dependent patient.

* * * * *

This patient was clearly a woman in conflict. Her alleged fear of hurting her husband was in stark conflict with her implicit wish to hurt her husband by engaging in an affair with his "best friend." Her fear (wish) of causing her husband's death was confirmed by Dr. Jackson who not only agreed that she had the power to do this but he also mandated that she change her behavior in order to prevent her husband's death. This apparent solution to her announced problem in no way addressed the underlying conflict which motivated her acting-out in her therapy with me and in her relationship with her husband's "friend."

In her therapy with me, as she gradually expressed less guilt and fear about her affair she also gradually appeared with less clothing. She transferred her verbal focus to nonverbal acting-out; that is, as she spoke less about her fear (wish) she became increasingly seductive. The intensity of her conflict was illustrated in her initial presentation when she made clear that her first choice of a therapist was someone whom she already knew, from her girlfriend's experience, would be a therapist who would be directive and authoritarian; that is, she knew that Dr. Jackson would insist that she not do what she feared she would wish to do. She knew she could avoid responsibility for her actions by letting him decide what she should do.

From the beginning of her sessions with me she secretly withheld the possibility that she had another therapy lined up as an escape clause from her therapy with me. When confronted by my comments about her "striptease," she avoided future sessions with me by quitting. In a sense, she acted out the rejection implicit in much of her behavior toward her husband. Her alleged "fear" of hurting him by her affair with his "friend" is analogous to her alleged fear that it would have been mean of her not to tell me in person that she was ending her therapy with me. Despite the rejection of her husband by having an affair and her rejection of me by changing therapists, she tells herself that she is being kind and not "mean."

Dr. Jackson reinforced her belief that she had a life-or-death power over her husband and then insisted she end her affair to prevent her husband's death. This may have intensified her basic conflict since the motivation which originally led her to begin the affair was never addressed.

Her repeated prolonged scrutiny of me, an apparent effort to evaluate who and what I was, was accompanied by her increasingly provocative dress, or lack of dress. When confronted, she terminated therapy, again in a challenging way. Unfortunately, her ambivalence and inner anger toward men remain untreated. With the collusion of her back-up directive therapist she withdrew from a therapy which might have led to real character change and not just superficial problem solving.

Despite her apparent passive submission to her directive therapist, there is some question, however, that this patient in truth was so passive, submissive and dependent. With a closer look, her behavior seems quite self-determined (albeit neurotic) and even manipulative in that she carefully evaluates the other person and probably predicts his response to her behavior. While she told me in our initial meeting that her preference was Dr. Jackson, she waited until our last session to report she had also been waiting for him to let her know when he had time to see her. With hindsight, I noted how convenient it was for her that he became available just when she wished to avoid confrontation of her own duplicitous behavior and could invoke her "escape clause."

Unfortunately, the apparent "escape" served to lock her in more strongly in the trap of her duplicity, fear and ambivalence which characterized so much of her behavior. This nice, punctual, kind, well-behaved woman who "innocently" was sexually provocative and "against her will" found herself having an affair which might kill her husband, to my knowledge, did not have a transforming therapy.

I regret I was unable to help this patient more. The mutual humanity in therapist and patient may well be the essential ingredient for effective psychotherapy and it may also sometimes interfere. I was not immune to her sexually provocative behavior and was probably less astute therapeutically in consequence. Only in hindsight did I see more clearly what her behavior was saying. Psychotherapy takes time. Both therapist and patient must be motivated to persist, and that is not always the case.

Patients usually come to psychotherapy for relief of symptoms and for help in solving their perceived problems and conflicts. They rarely come to be transformed or liberated from their lifelong dependent beliefs or freed from their restricting prejudices, biases and fallacious convictions. Therapists who offer patients only an authoritarian, directive, parental relationship may succeed in relieving symptoms, solving life problems and improving patients' social adjustments, but they will not liberate their patients from their basic dependency and lack of autonomy, or release their patients' potential to be creative and free spirits. Their patients will remain basically dependent people, vulnerable to relapse and recidivism. Only a therapy that seeks to free the human spirit has a chance to achieve such transformational goals.

Fortunately, a psychotherapy such as designed by Hellmuth Kaiser (Fierman, 1965) that offers a nondirective, nonauthoritarian, egalitarian relationship of communicative-intimacy between therapist and patient is such a therapy.

4

THE SEDUCTION OF DOCTOR NORTH

My psychoanalyst friend, Dr. Sidney Starr, referred Dr. Alexander North to me for psychotherapy. "Lou," he explained on the phone, "his ego is too fragile for analysis so I advised him to go to you first." I thought to myself, "These silly analysts think the only people suitable for psychoanalysis are those with 'strong' egos, whatever that means, while those with 'weak' egos are relegated to 'psychotherapy' which is supposed to be less stressful." Aloud, I responded, "Thanks, Sid. As soon as I fix his ego I'll send him back to you."

A week later North phoned and we arranged our first meeting. Alexander North was a short, stocky, balding 30-year-old, mild-mannered, bespectacled radiologist, living with his 62-year-old widowed mother and working full-time at a hospital in a nearby small Connecticut town. He entered my office hesitantly and went directly to the recliner facing mine. Without any prompting he began his story.

"I keep having this awful dream, Doctor Fierman, only it's more like an hallucination. The door to my bedroom opens, a bright light shines through and a huge hairy penis begins to come through the doorway. It almost fills the doorway and keeps coming into the room, and just as the rest of whatever it is seems about to come through I wake up in a cold sweat sitting upright in my bed. I'm afraid to go to sleep since the dream recurs about once a week. I decided to go to Sid Starr to be analyzed, but he told me I should have some regular therapy with you before I go into analysis with him." He was sweating profusely while telling his bizarre story. I silently wondered whether Starr might have been right about this man's ego.

"Perhaps your dream may be reflective of some serious stresses that might be troubling you these days."

North gulped, took a deep breath and said, "Stresses! Troubling me! Doctor, I'm in a terrible jam. I'm scheduled to get married in five months and I hardly know the girl, let alone love her. If I try to back out of it, she has three brothers who'd make Attila the Hun look like a choir boy. They already hate me for taking their little sister away from them, yet I'm sure they'd kill me if I didn't go through with it."

The rest of the session and for several weeks afterwards North filled his hours with details about his predicament. He had been in the last year of his residency training in radiology at a hospital in upstate New York. The chief of radiology's secretary was a tall, blond, willowy-shaped, 22-year-old beauty with a high school education who was courted by most of the male clinical staff in the hospital. While she dated many of the young doc-

tors, somehow her relationships never seemed to evolve
into anything more serious.

North finally joined his colleagues in asking for a
weekend date with Ingrid. After a movie they dined at a
local restaurant. "Doctor Fierman, I know it's hard to
believe, but I have no memory of what happened that
night. I know I have low tolerance for alcohol and I do
remember drinking wine during dinner, but after that—
nothing! All I know is that I woke the next morning with a
migraine headache and there was Ingrid in bed with me in
her apartment, hugging me and saying how much she
loved me and how happy she was that we were going to
get married!

"She made a point of telling me that she had already
phoned her family who lived nearby and that her mother
and three brothers were coming over that morning to
meet me! I panicked and told her that there was no way
that I would marry her and I hurriedly began to dress in
order to leave. She began to cry and warned me that her
family were devout Catholics and that her brothers would
kill her and me if they learned that we had sex without
intention to marry!

"What was I to do, Doc? What would you have done?
They came—the three brothers were huge dairy farmers—I was scared and when they all started pumping my
hand and pounding my back and hugging the breath out
of me—I felt helpless while Ingrid was telling them that
we would marry in December in Connecticut!

"Last month I finished my residency and started my
hospital job in my home town. My mother has met Ingrid
and likes her and has joined her in planning for a wedding
in our local church in December with a wedding party
afterward in our house."

With the exception of a few inquiries for clarification, I had remained essentially silent throughout the several sessions it took for him to complete his story. I noted silently that there had been no further reference to his nightmarish dream about a huge intruding penis, but I now assumed it represented his huge, threatening future brothers-in-law. "Alex," I said, "you look as if you are waiting for me to tell you what to do about your predicament. I can't do that. But I can tell you that it would be a travesty for you to go ahead with this marriage just because of fear and intimidation. I don't believe her brothers would kill her or you. Upset, yes—angry, yes—but homicidal, unlikely."

After a long silence North began to sob and in a low voice told me that his late father had abandoned him and his mother when he was five, and with clenched teeth he stated, "I've wanted to kill him ever since and I know those guys will want to kill me too."

The therapy remained at an impasse as the weeks moved inexorably toward the wedding date in December. I could not budge him from his passive resignation to his allegedly unwanted marriage. I suggested that Ingrid might be willing to reconsider if he at least told her that while he did not love her, he was committed to the marriage if she insisted. He reminded me that he had already done that and she seemed to ignore his plea while assuring him that she was certain she would make him happy to be with her once they were married. She persuaded him to have sex with her on her frequent visits and this seemed to lessen his despair a bit.

I finally conceded to myself that my patient was determined to go through with this marriage and that I should not try to dissuade him. Yet he seemed content to continue using his therapy with me in order to share his dread about the impending event. The weeks went by and finally the marriage was set for the following week. North told me he would be away for two weeks while honeymooning at Cape Cod after the wedding.

When he next appeared for his hour after the wedding he looked more depressed than ever. "The wedding party was awful," he broke out, "all those Swedish farmers carousing, guzzling beer and stuffing themselves, dancing with Ingrid and grabbing me to dance with them. I finally got a bottle of wine and went to my bedroom where I crawled out of the window into the back yard. I found a tree and sat down and leaned against it and finished off the bottle and fell asleep." He managed a sad smile and shook his head as he continued, "They finally noticed the groom was missing and began searching all over for me. Ingrid told me later that her brothers thought I had run away from home to get away from her, since they suspected that I didn't really want to marry her.

"At any rate they finally tracked me down and carried me half frozen back into the house and put me to bed. And now it's done and I'm married and I'm stuck for life. And to make matters worse she's now talking about babies."

"Alex," I countered, "you are a well-trained professional with a promising career. You are married to a beautiful woman whose main fault seems to be that she wanted to marry a doctor and be a housewife and mother. You report a gratifying sexual relationship with her. While love in marriage is ideal you should know that the success or failure of a marriage has more to do with mutuality, friendship and partnership of the relationship rather than the passion and romance that initiates most marriages. It's hard for me to believe that Ingrid can be truly happy with the situation as it is, since she must know how unhappy you are about it. I would suggest that you refer her to someone for individual psychotherapy and also arrange for some couples therapy either with her therapist or me or even a third therapist." North listened somberly and silently and ended the session with a terse statement, "I'll do it."

He later reported that his wife had also agreed and, at his request, I made arrangements for her to begin psychotherapy with a colleague of mine. A few weeks later North asked that I treat him and his wife together. Her therapist also agreed to her seeing me for their couples therapy. I cautioned them that Ingrid should understand that my primary allegiance was to Alex but that I would also try to be as helpful to her as I could.

In their couples therapy I was surprised to find that Ingrid was not only beautiful as described, but also showed a high level of intelligence, sensitivity, candor and compassionate affection for Alex. She reported that although her parents were uneducated immigrants and farmers, they were dedicated to the welfare of their children and had encouraged them to be independent and moral beings. She conceded that she wanted children very much and was quite discouraged by Alex's unwillingness. I found that the more I saw of them the more I felt allied to Ingrid's concerns and the less I felt supportive of Alex. She was clearly unhappy and I felt moved to try to be helpful to her.

"Alex," I said, "perhaps you would agree with the comedian, W. C. Fields, when he said, 'Anybody who hates children can't be all bad!' but I don't understand why you are so opposed to having children."

After several minutes of silence Alex responded, "My father was abusive to both me and my mother and then he left us when I was five. I wished I had a brother or even a sister. My mother refused to get a divorce and after my father died she rejected the few suitors who came around. I never had a sibling and envied my schoolmates who did. I never had a 'buddy' and was socially isolated throughout my childhood. It got so I disliked all the children my own age and now I still dislike kids, especially bratty ones."

Again I felt the therapy was at an impasse and I feared their precarious marriage would flounder unless I could get them to resolve the issue of having or not having children. We continued to meet weekly without much change until I was reminded of my Aunt Yetta, now long since dead.

She and my Uncle Dave had no children of their own and treated me and my siblings as if we were theirs. But they also had a cat, a friendly, frisky tabby cat. They doted on "Kitty," fed him gourmet food, brought him along whenever they visited, talked about him endlessly, recounting in boring detail all his latest tricks and adventures. After my uncle died Aunt Yetta became even more attached to Kitty, took him everywhere she went and conversed with him as if he understood everything she said and as if she knew everything he was thinking. When the inevitable happened and aging Kitty became ill and died my aunt became depressed and we children saw less and less of her until we learned several months later that she had died in her sleep. She was 70 and we were told she had died of a stroke but I knew she had really died of a heart broken by the loss of her beloved Kitty.

"That's it!' I thought, "Alex needs a pet." At our next session I deliberately inquired about Ingrid's childhood experiences. She spoke warmly about her family farm and the many animals there. As I anticipated, her parents also had many cats of several breeds and Ingrid was very fond of them.

"Do you miss them?" I asked innocently.

"Oh yes!" she replied enthusiastically, and turning to Alex she spoke the words I was telepathically trying to get her to say, "Oh Alex, as long as we're not going to have children, is it all right with you if we get a cat?"

"A cat! What a stupid idea!" he said.

"But Alex," I interjected, "a cat would keep Ingrid company while you were working at the hospital."

"Well," Alex groused, obviously feeling correctly that he was being ganged up on by both his wife and his therapist, "I never had pets and I don't like cats, but if that's what Ingrid wants, it's OK with me as long as I don't have to take care of it."

As therapy continued Ingrid proposed that she join the volunteer staff at Alex's hospital and this seemed to please Alex. She clearly and cleverly began to pursue the same interests that Alex had; namely art, classical music, golf, theater and travel. Their relationship gradually and pro-gressively moved toward becoming one of mutuality and friendship based on shared interests. And, meanwhile, there was Jezebel, their Himalayan cat.

Jezebel, they reported, was a beautiful Himalayan frisky kitten who seemed to prefer Alex as a playmate and would greet him whenever he returned home, jumping on his lap, nuzzling him to be petted, ever ready to play and fetch. Little by little Jezebel won Alex over, and it came as no surprise to me when they announced at their last session with me that Ingrid had become pregnant. Alex explained that they had finally decided to have a baby because they both agreed that Jezebel should have a companion and not be an "only child!"

* * * * *

In this therapy I deviated from the basic dictum of Kaiserian effective psychotherapy; namely, to be nondirective and focus solely and exclusively on offering an egalitarian relationship of communicative-intimacy. But to me Dr. North's case seemed to call for crisis intervention and marital counseling rather than a more ambitious curative psychotherapy. Therefore, I became more of an advisor, coach and avuncular therapist. Fortunately, it seemed to result in a happy outcome even though the therapy was somewhat manipulative and did not address the problem of Alex's basic dependency. I later heard from the Norths from time to time and there was no report of the clinical relapse which frequently occurs after directive psychotherapies. "In Medicine no one argues with success."

5

THE WOMAN WHO KILLED MARTIN LUTHER KING

The room was filled with friendly folk—talking, joking, laughing, introducing themselves to one another—drinking punch and munching on pretzels and potato chips. Fifteen psychiatrists from various Northern states were meeting that evening of April 4, 1968 in Montgomery, Alabama with a group of social workers from local community social service agencies. The psychiatrists were here as part of a government grant to learn about mental illness and mental health services in a Southern city.

The plan that evening was for each psychiatrist to meet with an assigned Montgomery social worker and then to spend the following day with him or her observing the services being provided by that worker's agency. Most of the social workers were black and most were women. A party spirit prevailed and we psychiatrists basked in the warmth of Southern hospitality and interracial friendship. A black man suddenly entered the room, agitated and distraught. He sought out the leader of the gathering and whispered something in his ear. The leader looked stunned and then called out loudly: "Friends! Please! May I have your attention! I have just received terrible news! Martin Luther King has been assassinated in Memphis!"

Pandemonium broke out. Most of the psychiatrists were shocked and speechless. Many of the social workers screamed and wept. We tried to comfort one another. After several minutes had passed the leader again called out, "Friends, I think we should end our party now. You all know where to meet in the morning. Unless you hear otherwise we will carry out the program as planned." I headed out of the room into the hallway of the hotel where the party had been held. I happened to be the last to leave when suddenly the leader came out and rushed up to me: "Doctor! Please come with me! We have an emergency!"

He led me into a side room. There a few social workers were attempting to physically restrain a struggling weeping woman. I was told that she was Patricia Parsons, Ph.D., a divorced single mother of a three-year-old son, professor of social work at the local university, prominent in local politics and with no known history of past mental illness. She was a tall, beautiful, well dressed, black woman thrashing about trying to free herself from her colleagues. I intervened and signaled the others to release her. Once freed she began to pace feverishly about the room, wringing her hands, pulling at her hair, alternately sobbing and then crying out: "Oh God! Oh God all mighty! God all mighty! I've killed Martin Luther King! I've killed Martin Luther King!"

I paced alongside her. "No, no, Doctor Parsons. You did not kill Martin Luther King." I hoped my soft-spoken assurances would calm her but to no avail. Back and forth she paced and her weeping and repetitive protestations only seemed to increase in intensity the more I tried to comfort her. "This woman is having an acute reactive paranoid psychosis," I thought to myself. "I'm going to have to hospitalize her if her delusional disorder doesn't subside soon or if she becomes suicidal."

I asked one of the bystanders to take my place and to continue walking with her while I spoke to her worried friends. "She's obviously very upset over King's death," I said, "but I hope she will feel better in the morning." I advised that they take her home and arrange to have someone stay with her through the night. I prescribed some Valium and asked that I be called at my hotel if things got worse and to let me know in the morning how she was doing. I cautioned that if she did not recover overnight she would probably have to be hospitalized.

Doctor Parsons went along with her friends, weeping and moaning about killing Reverend King. I and my fellow psychiatrists returned to our hotel where we were cautioned not to leave the hotel that night. Soon the city erupted with rioting by blacks venting their anger and grief by burning buildings, shooting and assaulting whites, storming and looting white-run stores. We all feared for our own safety and spent a fitful night.

Early next morning I was phoned in my room and told that someone wanted to see me in the lobby. I went down and there was Doctor Parsons, smiling, alert, calm and composed and clearly not psychotic! "Thank you, Doctor Fierman, for trying to help me last night," she said. "I'm sure you must have thought I was insane!"

"Well, that did cross my mind," I said. We found a bench to sit and talk. "Let me explain," she said. "A black state congressman is running for governor of Alabama in the upcoming election. One month ago I organized a rally on his behalf to take place yesterday in Montgomery. Reverend King was then in Memphis to support the garbage men's strike for better working conditions there. I called Reverend King in Memphis to plead with him to come to Montgomery yesterday to speak at my rally and he agreed. Well, yesterday morning he called to say that negotiations in the Memphis strike had reached a critical point and, although he was willing to honor his commitment to speak at our rally here if we held him to it, he asked if I would please release him from his promise and cancel his appearance here so that he could continue his efforts to help the garbage men there in Memphis . . . Don't you see? If only I had held him to his commitment to be here yesterday he would not have been killed!" She began to sob quietly as she finished her story. "No, Doctor Parsons," I said. "The only difference would have been that his assassin would have followed him here and he would have been shot in Montgomery instead of Memphis. You did not kill Martin Luther King!" Still sobbing she nodded her head in agreement.

* * * * *

The discerning therapist should never dismiss delusional statements of patients as being totally meaningless, but instead should search patiently for their hidden relevance. There is always a kernel of truth in the delusions of psychotic people just as there is always some measure of reality in our dreams, no matter how disguised or distorted. What seemed at first to be a bizarre distortion of reality in this historical instance became an understandable, albeit unjustified, misinterpretation of facts once the facts were known.

6

YOU'D BE PARANOID TOO IF EVERYONE WERE AGAINST YOU

This is the story of a paranoid schizophrenic patient whom I have been treating for the past eight years. Gradually, over the years I heard less and less from him about persecutory delusions, and now for the past two years he seems completely free of any delusions or other signs of thought disorder. Throughout his psychotherapy with me he firmly refused any psychotropic medication.

Jozeph Kerenski was a 60-year-old, married, unemployed Polish immigrant, referred to me by his chiropractor who had heard of me from other patients of his. At our first meeting he proved to be a short, wiry, casually dressed, intense, gray-haired man who strode into my office, thrust out his hand for a handshake and, in broken English with a heavy Polish accent, said, "My name is Jozeph Kerenski and somebody's trying to kill me!"

Jozeph went on to explain that for several years he was being painfully "zapped" by laser beams aimed at his back, stomach and genitals. He attributed these beams as coming from a hostile witch. His family doctor found no organic pathology to account for the pains so Jozeph finally sought help from his chiropractor who persuaded him to see me. I suggested antipsychotic medication but he adamantly refused. "I don't need pills. I need help to stop these beams before they kill me."

"Look, Jozeph," I said, "I don't believe such a thing as being tortured by laser beams is possible, but since you are having pain that doctors seem unable to explain or treat, I would agree with your chiropractor that psychiatric treatment may be of help." And so began a psychotherapy that has continued over the past eight years. In therapy he has always been active, filling his hours with vivid accounts of laser beams aimed at him from a distance and penetrating his body, usually at night, causing pain in his back, chest, abdomen and groin.

I listened passively and chose not to challenge his delusional talk but, instead, conveyed my interest in everything and anything he chose to bring to his therapy hours. His life history gradually emerged haphazardly over the weeks and months. He did not know who his father was. He was born in a small farming village near Warsaw. His teenage mother brought him to the village convent and he was raised by the nuns there. He attended a local school but left after the sixth grade and worked as the convent gardener. As a teenager he became sexually active with girls from the village. At age 18 he was drafted into the Polish army and although he did not experience combat he was kept in a military prisoner camp for two years after the Nazis overran Poland. When released he returned to the convent as its gardener. A marriage broker sought him out to arrange a marriage with an American-Polish woman who was seeking a husband. She came by plane to Poland, married him and they then returned to her home in New Haven, Connecticut. They had three children, now grown and living separately. But when they were small he worked in a local garden nursery while his wife worked as an office clerk in a local department store. To help care for their children her widowed mother had moved in with them.

"Doctor, she turned out to be the witch!" he proclaimed several months into his therapy. He reported that while his mother-in-law was living with them she would entice him to come into her bedroom when his wife was away and would have forcible sex with him. If he resisted or refused he noticed he would suffer afterwards with sharp pains in his body. "I had to give in. Otherwise she would zap me with laser beams," he groaned, "until I finally insisted that my wife send her away to live with one of her sisters. That was three years ago but since then she has been zapping me every night."

The weeks and months went by and while his hours always included reports of being "zapped," his demeanor gradually changed. He became more relaxed, more cheerful, more lighthearted and more willing to discuss a wide range of other topics and themes: his life history, army experiences, his children and grandchildren, his pet dog, his garden and his marriage. Gradually there was less and less reporting of torture by laser beams and finally all such references ceased completely. Throughout this period I elected to make no inquiries about his disappearing paranoid delusion but remained interested in any and all topics he brought to his hours.

Two years ago he suffered a heart attack while working in his garden and underwent by-pass surgery. His surgery and post-operative rehabilitation interrupted his psychotherapy for about three months and when he returned he requested monthly sessions instead of weekly. The hours are lively and he seems happy to come and reluctant to leave. There is no sign of delusional paranoid thinking and I have made no inquiry about it. I remain content to meet with him as long as he wishes to continue his friendly encounters with me and I regard his therapy now as justified in that it is preventing his relapse into his former paranoid state.

* * * * *

In this age of psychopharmacotherapy and electroconvulsive shock therapy clinicians may forget that in previous years, when such therapies were not available, psychotic patients in mental hospitals received little more than staff-patient psychosocial interactions. Nonetheless, the spontaneous remission and discharge rate was about 60% within the first year of hospitalization, usually followed by relapses in subsequent years. There is also the occasional phenomenon of chronic, paranoid, delusional psychotic patients experiencing a gradual spontaneous remission after several decades of mental disability.

For a more detailed discussion of the psychotherapy of schizophrenia, see *The Therapist Is the Therapy* (Fierman, 1997). In regard to the frequency of therapy sessions or the duration of therapy, there is no absolute rule. The therapist must use judgment not to foster dependency by prolonging therapy unnecessarily but also not to reject the patient arbitrarily because of some symptomatic improvement. This man's blatant paranoid comments gradually stopped as his therapy progressed, and he finally requested less frequent meetings, which currently seems appropriate. Other patients might terminate therapy and then return periodically, every six months or every year for brief visits. A therapist should remain flexible and open to what is appropriate or "works" for each person.

This patient's life experiences were heavily weighted with controlling women, from his mother (no known father) to convent nuns to a wife (plus her mother) who brought him to a new and strange country. For him to find a separate, non-controlling, male friend (therapist) was a factor in the remission of his psychosis, and that relationship should not be terminated unilaterally by the therapist because of the risk of relapse.

7

CATATONIA

Jefferson Turner and his wife, Dolly, were driving leisurely on a country road near Jackson, Mississippi where he was attending a meeting at his corporation headquarters. They drove by a large field where several black men and women were picking cotton.

"Look at those blacks, Dolly," he snarled, "working their asses off picking cotton and glad to have a job, even for minimum wage, while my damn niggers back in Connecticut are always bellyaching for more pay and threatening to close down the factory."

Dolly was silent while Jeff continued his strident tirade, but it grated on her and finally she broke out, "Jeff, before the Civil War the South enslaved the blacks and ever since the Civil War you racists have been exploiting them both in the South and the North."

Jeff swerved the car to the side of the road and slammed on the brakes. "Damn it!" he shouted, "I've had it with your fucking Liberal bullshit!" Sputtering and fuming he leaned over and jerked open the passenger door. "Once and for all, Dolly, either button your lip and keep your Commy bullshit to yourself or you can damn well get out and walk and keep walking!"

This was the story told to me by my patient, Dolly Turner, as she waited with me for her husband to come to the hospital and sign her out "A.M.A." (against medical advice). She had been admitted to the psychiatric service ten days before. Her history had been provided by her husband. Dolly was 31 years old, Catholic, lived with her husband in a Connecticut town near her husband's manufacturing factory. He was 58 years old and CEO of the plant. They had been married seven years, no children, her first and his second marriage. She had been his private secretary for a year before she consented to an affair with him after he promised to divorce his 49-year-old wife of twenty years.

On her admission Mr. Turner claimed that his wife seemed well until a week before when they returned from a meeting of his in Mississippi. He then noticed that she became increasingly uncommunicative and withdrawn. On the morning of admission he was alarmed when she refused to get out of bed or speak to him at all. Instead, she simply lay stiffly in her bed staring at the ceiling. He called their family doctor who advised that she be taken by ambulance to the hospital. Mr. Turner made no mention of the quarrel in Mississippi about which she told me ten days later.

On admission she proved to be an attractive, healthy looking, dark-haired woman, with no abnormal findings on physical or neurological examination, but she would not move or speak. She was stiff and robot-like and maintained any position or posture in which she was physically placed. In short, she presented as a flexible statue, all the while staring blankly ahead. The diagnosis was clearly acute catatonia.

Catatonia is a state of being first described by Kahlbaum (1874). The catatonic patient is mute and passively maintains his limbs in any position in which they are placed no matter how grotesque. The patient submits to spoonfeeding or is fed forcibly by stomach tube. The condition is usually associated with schizophrenia and responds poorly to treatment including electro-shock therapy and psychopharmacotherapy. However, in rare cases the patient recovers spontaneously and without other manifestations of schizophrenia.

I was familiar with a clinical report of the psychotherapy of a catatonic patient by Robert Knight, M.D. (1946), in which he more or less carried a catatonic adolescent boy outdoors from the hospital onto the surrounding grounds and then, while pulling the boy along as they walked, Dr. Knight maintained a monologue throughout the session. After a few weeks the boy gradually began to move spontaneously and to speak to Dr. Knight and went on to a complete recovery.

I decided to try this approach rather than subject Mrs. Turner to shock therapy or psychiatric drugs. The nurses dressed her each morning, spoon-fed her, tended to her personal hygiene and then stood her up like a dress-shop manikin in the doorway of her room. Each day I would arrive at the designated hour, take her by the arm and gently guide her off the ward to the small outdoor clearing encircled by the hospital buildings where we would walk for about an hour. Following are some samples of my many monologues during the daily therapy hour with Dolly:

• "Dolly, I trust you can hear me and understand me. I appreciate your willingness to walk with me during our therapy hours. I hope that sooner or later you will decide to speak to me and move around the way you usually do. You must know that this is a psychiatric hospital where people come to be helped with their emotional and psychological troubles. I'm a psychiatrist and my name is Dr. Fierman. Your husband told me that after you returned from Mississippi, you became uncommunicative and withdrawn and finally stopped moving or talking and your family doctor advised that you be brought here."

• "You look to me as if you have frozen yourself out of fear, like a deer or rabbit that freezes when it senses that great danger will occur if it even moves or makes a sound. I know you must have a good reason for behaving this way and I hope I can relieve your fear that something catastrophic will happen if you move or speak."

• "You are a beautiful young woman and your husband has told me the story of his falling in love with you while you were his secretary and how he divorced his wife in order to marry you. But I sense there is trouble there for you. He is almost twice your age and probably doesn't share all your beliefs and values. He spoke of you with much caring and affection, but clearly it looks like some alienation has occurred between the two of you. Perhaps you are trying to protect him in some magical way by freezing and being mute. There is an old saying that 'words can kill' and you may be afraid that it can be literally true."

• "Dolly, you have locked yourself within yourself; you've turned away from life and time and relationships, stopping the world and choosing a living death. You're too young to reject life no matter how badly life has treated you so far. You have a long future ahead, full of adventure and surprises and love and passion and mystery. Of course there will be bad times, maybe even worse than whatever has happened to you recently, but there will be good times too for you to enjoy with or without your husband. Don't despair—don't give up on life—come out of your prison—live dangerously—come back—come back!"

My exhortations seemed to have fallen on deaf ears as the week came to an end. Away from the hospital, during the weekend, I resigned myself to the conclusion that my efforts had been in vain and that I would have to resort to psychopharmacological drugs and possibly electro-convulsive shock therapy to try to bring her out of her catatonia. But to my surprise when I arrived Monday morning she was in her room, smartly dressed, fully made-up and smiling. She greeted me with a warm embrace and bubbling words of appreciation!

"Thank you, Dr. Fierman, for all you've done for me, but now I'm well again and I've called my husband and he's on his way here to take me home."

"But—but Dolly!" I protested, "how can you simply leave like this? You've been very ill and we need to find out what's happened to you and make sure it doesn't happen again."

"No, Doctor, that won't be necessary," she said firmly.

"But Dolly, why didn't you move or speak?"

"All right," she said, "I'll try to explain while we're waiting for my husband."

She went on to tell me the story of her husband's angry outburst and his brutal ultimatum when they were in Mississippi. "He told me to 'button my lip—or else!'" she said, "and I was very angry with him and became frightened that I might do him some harm. Gradually I felt I had to be completely silent and not speak or move. I knew that, somehow, if I did speak or move something terrible would happen to my husband and he would be destroyed! I know you think that's crazy, but it's true."

"And how do you know it's true?" I said.

"It was just a very strong feeling. I don't know how or why. I just knew that if I moved or spoke, my husband would die. Your being with me and talking to me the way you did helped the fear go away and this morning I felt normal again, thanks to you."

"But are you sure you want to leave and go back to your husband?"

"Yes, even though Jeff's a bigot, I've forgiven him for threatening me."

"Dolly, I'm sorry but I don't believe you at all. Excuse me for being so blunt and confronting but I can't simply let you leave without letting you know how concerned I am about your mental state and how precarious your sanity is. I suspect you were gravely upset by his crude racist outburst in Mississippi because, for some reason, you identify with the black slaves of history. Isn't that true, Dolly? Aren't you in fact a slave yourself?"

Dolly blanched and stared at me, looking frightened.

"Forgive me, Dolly. I don't usually talk this way to my patients but, as I said, I'm worried that you may relapse into a psychotic state unless you face the truth about yourself and your relationship to your husband."

"Dr. Fierman," she whispered, "I'm black myself! I'm a light-skinned black and no one knows it now but you.

My grandmother was white and after I went to secretarial school in Alabama I came North and got this job. Jeff hit on me almost immediately and he's so rich and my family was so poor I accepted him. I told him I was an orphan raised by nuns and he believed me. I'm careful not to get pregnant because I'm afraid my child will be black."

"But how can you live this way, Dolly, your whole life is a lie."

"I can and I will and I trust you not to betray me."

Mr. Turner arrived and curtly dismissed my efforts to have them reconsider her sudden departure. I warned them that she was in danger of having a relapse or some other related mental disorder and urged that she see a psychiatrist, but they both disagreed and left.

I learned a year or so afterward that they had moved to Mississippi where Mr. Turner assumed a higher executive position in his corporation. There was no word of any recurrence of Mrs. Turner's delusional catatonia.

* * * * *

The mechanism for this patient's sudden recovery in this instance appears to have been my persistent psychotherapeutic effort maintained in spite of her apparent lack of response, and she herself attributed her recovery to this. However, the dynamics are far from clear since the psychohistory facts of her life are not completely known. All we know is that this patient presented an obvious catatonic state and after one week of concentrated one-sided psychotherapy there was a dramatic reversal with complete absence of catatonia.

Diagnostically I regard Mrs. Turner as either a delusional hysteric or an atypical catatonic schizophrenic with a circumscribed delusional system involving magical powers. Her beauty, intelligence and affable personality seemed to provide her with a somewhat protective veneer of normalcy. But as this episode demonstrated, she was either living with a devastating secret or a remarkable fantasy and would continue to be vulnerable to having a psychotic reaction when confronted with extreme stress.

8

THE RELUCTANT
WIFE-BEATER

Morris Cohen, Doctor of Chiropractic Medicine, leaned forward in the lounge chair facing me, wringing his hands and sweating profusely. "Doctor!" he pleaded, "You've got to help me. I'm afraid I'm going to kill my wife. Just like my friend Jack Burlowe did a week ago. You must have read about it in the papers" (I had not). "He beat her to death accidentally. I mean he didn't mean to kill her but he knocked her down and she hit her head on the fireplace and died. I'm afraid that's going to happen with me and Esther too. She's constantly fighting with me about everything and then I lose my temper and smack her and down she goes. Then I start crying and try to pick her up and tell her how sorry I am, but she doesn't buy it and tells me what a shmuck I am and it starts all over again. Sometimes I hit her a second time in the same argument and once even a third time. She sticks her chin right in my face

and dares me to hit her and then—Bam!—I smack her and
down she goes again. I'm afraid; some day she won't be
able to get up again and she'll be dead because I killed
her." He covered his face in his hands and shook his head
and rocked back and forth, moaning.

"I agree with you, Doctor Cohen." I said, "This is
indeed a very a serious problem. Assaulting your wife
endangers both your wife and yourself and it's good that
you've decided to go into therapy." He agreed to weekly
sessions.

Morris was forty-five years old, married fifteen years,
two sons, age fourteen and ten. He had a thriving chiropractic practice in a nearby suburb. He was a burly
muscular man, obviously capable of inflicting serious
damage on either an opponent or a victim. He spent
several sessions reviewing his history. He was the oldest
of five children of Russian immigrant Jewish parents who
settled in Long Island. His father was a tailor, his mother
a housewife. She was domineering and critical of her
husband and they quarreled frequently and on occasion
came to blows. Morris was a street brawler as a teenager
and briefly considered boxing as a possible career. He did
well in school and became a pre-med student at City
College in New York, but failed to gain acceptance into a
medical school. Chiropractic training school was a second choice and after graduation his private practice in
suburban Connecticut flourished.

Morris reported that although he had a few intimacies
with women along the way he had no serious attachments
until friends of his parents finally arranged a meeting for
him with their daughter, Esther. She was an attractive
twenty-nine-year-old office secretary with a history of
alienating all her previous suitors with her aggressive
scorn and sarcasm. "I think she was nice to me," Morris

speculated, "because she was getting worried about her chances of finding a husband, so she curbed her nastiness until after our honeymoon in Bermuda. After that it was like Shakespeare's *Taming of the Shrew*, only I never tamed her."

"You seem to have a flip way of telling a sad story, Morris," I said, "but I suspect you were and still are very unhappy and disappointed with your marriage." He nodded sadly and added that their sexual life had also deteriorated with rare occurrences only at her initiative.

"You haven't said when and why you started hitting her." (*Kaiserian therapists are nondirective and tend to avoid direct questioning of their patients. Questions give the patient the option of being either compliant or noncompliant, in either case the patient's dependency is reinforced by having the therapist's question determine his responsive behavior. The therapist can better get the information he is seeking simply by making a statement or observation about the issue at hand rather than by asking a question.*)

"Well, Esther turned out to be even more domineering and critical than my own mother, and I guess I was a passive, hen-pecked husband until about two years ago when my son came to me. He was twelve then and told me he had been listening to my wife's phone calls on the extension phone in his room. He told me that Esther's mother would phone Esther every day while I was at my office and my son secretly would listen in on his grandmother's calls.

"He reported that she usually would start the conversation by saying, '*Nu*, so what's your *momzer* husband up to now?' *Momzer* is a Yiddish word for bastard or an untrustworthy and bad character, and my wife would laugh and say what a shmuck I was and how she could get me to do anything she wanted. That did it, and the next time she started to run me down I smacked her. But it hasn't scared her off and only made things worse. She's after me just about every day, complaining, nagging, haranguing until I lose it and hit her and then she stops for about a day or so."

"You look pretty powerful to me," I commented, "but you haven't mentioned any injuries that your wife must get when you hit her."

"Well, actually, I think I must hold back at the last moment when I punch her, because, other than a few bruises on her face, she hasn't had any injuries. No bleeding or broken bones, so far.

"We've talked about divorce but we both agreed to wait until the children get older. I don't think the kids would want to live with her. Especially my older son who keeps listening to his mother's phone calls and reporting them to me."

"It does sound as if you approve of your son's listening to other people's phone calls."

Morris shrugged and went on with his weekly reporting of his latest quarrel with his wife. Listening to my patient's lament week after week I found myself vacillating between feeling worried that he might seriously injure his wife and feeling sorry for this unhappy man's lonely and loveless marriage. He clearly had a love/hate relationship with Esther. I had suggested couples therapy. He agreed but reported that she refused.

I became increasingly aware that the therapy seemed to have bogged down. Morris's violent outbursts continued at least once a month and I worried that he might yet inflict more serious injuries. His son's eavesdropping on his wife's phone calls continued to fuel his rage and Morris's behavior both in and out of his sessions seemed unchanged and unaffected by his ongoing therapy. I then decided that the urgency of Morris's family situation warranted directive, confrontative crisis-intervention therapy rather than continued nondirective, long-term, cure-oriented psychotherapy.

"Listen, Morris," I finally said, "I don't think it's healthy or moral for your son to keep spying on his mother and grandmother on your behalf and with your encouragement. I believe you and he would both feel better if you told him to stop." Morris reluctantly agreed and later reported that his son had promised to cease his sneaky activity.

Finally, after listening to Morris's anguished report of another quarrel with his wife ending with his assault followed by his tearful apologies spurned by his scornful wife, I declared, "Morris, in no way do I condone your hitting your wife and you simply must stop doing that. There is simply no justification for your assaultive behavior with Esther. But I've also been wondering whether there may be more to it than your simply having a violent dangerous temper. I suspect it may be more complex than that."

"I don't understand, Doc." Morris said. "What are you driving at?"

"Well, look. You've already told me that you used to be passive and hen-pecked with Esther. Is it possible that you are still being passive and compliant with her even in your hitting her?"

"Come off it, Doc. That's ridiculous."

"Listen, Morris. I suspect that your wife may want you to hit her and that you are simply complying with her desire to control and dominate you. She sets you up to hit her, knowing now that you are careful not to injure her seriously. She can then control you by shaming you. She maintains moral superiority over you in your family and in your relationship with her. And she seems willing to pay the price of being slightly beaten because this makes it possible for her to maintain controlling power over you. She may also be motivated to establish a record of your violence to present to a divorce court in the future"

Morris received my exhortations with wide-eyed rapt attention. After a few minutes of silence he proclaimed, "I need some time to think about what you are saying to me about her. On the one hand it sounds crazy, but on the other hand it feels like there's a ring of truth to it. The way she sticks her chin in my face. It's almost like she's really asking me to hit her."

The next session he appeared excited and announced, "By God, you're right! She's been asking for it right along and I've been falling for it and living like a damned rotten wife-beater begging for her forgiveness!" He seemed elated to have a new liberating perspective of his own hitherto self-despised behavior. Subsequent therapy hours were replete with reports of Esther trying in vain to provoke Morris into violence. "You would have been proud of me, Doc." he boasted, "I kept my cool even when she shoves her chin right into my face, calls me a 'momzer'; and get this, Doc, she even punched me in the face, but I wouldn't retaliate. It was 'turn the other cheek' time for me, and I shamed her far worse than she has ever done me."

Soon he reported that Esther, completely frustrated over his ignoring her provocations, had finally asked for a divorce and they began the necessary proceedings. When the two sons declared their desire to live with their father, Esther moved out and went to live with her mother on Long Island. Morris continued his therapy for several weeks more, noteworthy in that he began courting a nurse he had met. He subsequently terminated his therapy and married the nurse with the enthusiastic encouragement of his two sons. I heard from him a few times over the years and there were no reports of any recurrence of violent behavior.

* * * * *

Spousal violence usually involves couples caught up in a sado-masochistic relationship. Paradoxically, these relationships are frequently long-lasting. While the parties involved may rationalize their remaining in the relationship as being unavoidable, unchangeable or inescapable, to the observer these are only lame and dubious excuses for indulging their own sadism and self-hatred. Spousal violence also seems to have a built-in escalating propensity, leading to the ever increasing danger of more and more serious disabling injuries and even death.

In the case of Morris, therapeutic crisis-intervention aborted the cycle of escalating spousal violence. He became able to reframe his perspective in terms of the provocations by his wife. This freed him from compulsive compliance with his wife's efforts to keep him trapped in the shameful role of wife-beater.

However, his wife's apparent manipulativeness in no way freed him from responsibility for his own violence. The underlying anger in Morris was implicit in his claiming he was more or less seduced into marriage by his duplicitous wife who had concealed her "nastiness" and "shrewishness" until after they were married.

While the therapy did not deal with the underlying motivating factors in Morris himself which contributed to his violence and to his deteriorating relationship with his wife, it did make escape possible for both him and his wife.

9

GO AND
SIN NO MORE

Helen Marlowe was 28, average height and weight, simply dressed, brunette, moderate make-up and jewelry, with a bruised black eye and obviously distraught, wringing her hands and dabbing at her tears with tissues, having trouble speaking between sobs.

"Doctor! I'm afraid he'll find out I'm here and then he'll beat me again!" She had called early that afternoon to say it was an emergency and urgent that she see someone that day. I had agreed to meet with her at the end of my scheduled day.

"Take your time and calm down, Miss Marlowe. There's no hurry and you are my last patient of the day."

After several minutes elapsed she began her story. "This man I live with—Joe—he has a terrible temper—and he's very irritable and he drinks—and it's gotten so that I hate him but I'm afraid to leave—he's threatened to kill me if I try to leave or if I go to the police."

We both agreed that the protective services offered to battered women by police or court injunctions were unreliable as evidenced by repeated newspaper reports of women assaulted or even killed despite court restraining orders and police notification. "Well, Miss Marlowe," I finally said, "I'm not sure psychotherapy will solve your problem, but it should help you deal with this man more effectively." We arranged to meet weekly.

Over the next several weeks Helen revealed that she and her brother had been raised in foster homes, her parents having been killed in a car accident when she was eight. Her foster parents were strict Catholics and harsh disciplinarians who resorted to physical punishment for any misconduct. Her brother ran away when he was fifteen and now lived in a small oil town in Texas. She was a school drop-out and, as an adolescent, became part of a wild, undisciplined group of teenagers who indulged in alcohol, marihuana, promiscuous sex, vandalism and petty crime. At eighteen she left her foster home to live with the leader of the group, the man with whom she was still living ten years later. The two of them both worked on the assembly line at a local manufacturing factory.

"Joe was good to me the first few years we lived together, but his drinking and hanging out with his buddies bothered me and I used to nag at him about it and he started hitting me, particularly when he had been drinking. It's gotten worse and lately he drinks every day and hits me even when I haven't done or said anything."

I was puzzled by several things in her narrative and finally commented, "You've made it quite clear that you're very unhappy about your relationship with Joe, but, somehow, you never say why you stayed with him all these years after he began to beat you."

"Well, for one, he's usually sorry afterwards and tries to make up for his violence—buys me presents and apologizes; and for two, his salary added to mine makes it possible for us to live better than we could alone; and for three, we're sort of common-law married and I am Catholic and Catholics are not supposed to get divorced; and, finally, as I told you, he says he'll kill me if I try to leave him."

"Helen," I said, "it doesn't sound to me as if you yourself believe what you are saying. There must be some other reason or reasons why you would stay so long with such an abusive and dangerous person." Helen became agitated at my words and said petulantly as the hour ended, "Well, if you think I'm a liar, that's your problem."

And then it happened again. Helen appeared battered, both eyes blackened, wearing dark sunglasses, trying with difficulty to speak between sobs, "He was drunk at dinner and got mad because I picked up the phone when it rang instead of letting the call go through to our answering machine . . . and when I started talking to my girlfriend . . . he started choking me and punching me in the face . . . and screaming he was going to kill me."

I waited for her crying to subside and then exhorted her, "Helen, why do you put up with this? Why don't you leave him? He may or may not kill you if you leave, but it is certain he will kill or maim you if you stay. You must leave!"

Helen stared at me, wide-eyed at my emotional plea. Then, with tears flowing, she bowed her head and whispered, "Doctor, you don't understand. I can't leave because I'm getting just what I deserve! This is my punishment—my penance." She began moaning and swaying back and forth. "I did it—I murdered my baby—this is my punishment!"

I was dumbfounded. "What are you saying! What baby! What murder! What are you talking about?"

"When I was seventeen I was sleeping around and I got pregnant. . . . I didn't even know which of the guys I hung out with was the father. . . . I was afraid to tell my foster parents and I scraped up enough money to go to an unlicensed doctor for an illegal abortion. . . . I killed my baby!"

"Helen! That was eleven years ago. Don't you go to church? Haven't you gone to confession or talked to your priest?"

"No. I still go to Mass regularly but I've been too ashamed to go to confession and tell my priest about my abortion or my living with Joe."

"Helen, I've got a good friend who is a Jesuit priest. I'd like you to go and see him and talk to him about your abortion. I'm sure he will help you with your guilty feelings about it." Helen agreed and I gave her my friend's telephone number.

The following week Helen appeared radiant and beaming and said breathlessly, "I saw Father Scott and he told me that my guilty suffering over the years was more than enough penance for my abortion and he gave me absolution for my sin. But he said I was living in sin with Joe and I should either leave him or marry him which I would never do, so I'm going to leave him as soon as I can figure out a way to do it without getting killed."

"It sounds like Father Scott has told you to 'go and sin no more' just like the Bible says Jesus told Mary Magdalene."

Her euphoria over feeling freed from her burden of chronic guilt gradually dissipated as she took inventory of her skills and assets. "I've never been completely on my own and I don't even have a high school diploma," she complained.

"But you know as well as I do that there are courses available for adults who want an equivalent diploma."

"Yes, but I'm afraid I'll fail at it."

"Well, one sure way to avoid failure is not to try."

"You're mean. Why don't you be more encouraging."

"Like Father Scott?"

"Yes—why not?"

"Because I'm not Father Scott. Besides, I am encouraging you in my own way. I'm sure you'll do well and the diploma will help you get better jobs than the one you have."

Helen did complete a high school equivalency course and then went on to a secretarial school. Meanwhile, she was extra careful not to provoke her consort and was able to avoid beatings. In a few months she seemed to have become transformed from a mousy, dependent, guilt-ridden, fearful woman to a cocky, confident, cheerful woman, eagerly plotting her escape from her brutal and threatening consort.

"I've called my brother in Texas and told him the whole story and he's agreed that I should join him there. He's sure he can help me find a job. Joe doesn't know about my brother in Texas because I never told him. So I've decided to leave Connecticut next Wednesday when Joe plans to spend the day fishing with his drinking buddies. I've made all the arrangements to quit my job and they've promised not to tell Joe where I'm going. My girlfriend will take care of my dog. So, 'Doc,' I guess this is my last session with you. Thanks for everything. I'll write to you."

As I said good-bye and wished her well, I closed with my usual, "You know I'll always be as close to you as the telephone." I have received happy letters from her from time to time, the last time announcing her marriage to a Texas oil worker.

* * * * *

The Catholic Church having first condemned abortion as a mortal sin has also devised a mechanism for relieving devastating guilt; namely, confession, penance and absolution. Psychotherapy can also provide the benefits of confession and convert guilt, which by its very nature is neurotic self-blame, into nonself-blaming remorseful regret. But psychotherapy cannot provide the absolution needed to relieve the guilt of a religious True Believer. Here, collaboration between religion and psychotherapy is useful.

Fortunately, in this instance, I knew a priest to whom I could refer the patient for spiritual help and religious guidance; and he did, in fact, help her abandon the self-torture she was accepting as punishment because of her own belief in guilt for her sins. The apparent happy outcome seems due in part to effective psychotherapy and effective pastoral counseling and in part to the patient's ability to respond by taking effective charge of her own life.

10

A BOND OF
MUTUAL LOATHING

"Now look. This simply won't do. Someone has to take this fellow. We can't deny him therapy just because he's a damn Nazi!" Thus spake Dr. Carl Greenfield, chief of the out-patient psychiatric clinic at the Yale-New Haven Hospital where I was serving my second year of residency training in the Yale Department of Psychiatry.

It was the daily Intake Meeting of the clinical staff where decisions were made as to who would be the psychotherapist for each new patient applying or referred for therapy. Dr. Greenfield wanted staff members to volunteer for each new patient rather than assign them arbitrarily or in rotation. He thought that would make for a better "match" between patient and therapist. He would present the staff with whatever information he had about the patient and then ask for a volunteer—and that was the problem in this case. Dr. Greenfield had informed the six of us on his staff that the patient was a 29-year-old, German-born, unabashed anti-Semitic Nazi sympathizer. When Greenfield called for a volunteer therapist, the clinical staff responded with deafening silence.

The year was 1951, six years since the end of World War II, two years since the end of the Nuremberg trials and three years since the founding of Israel, a homeland for the survivors of the Holocaust. I had always identified with the Jewish victims of persecution and anti-Semitism throughout history and throughout the world.

Suddenly, to my own surprise and dismay, I heard myself saying, "I'll take him!" I felt strangely detached and could see, as if from a distance, my colleagues staring at me in amazement while Dr. Greenfield, beaming with approval, handed me the patient's file. As he began presenting other patients, I reflected on my impulsive act. Why had I done it? Was it grandstanding, trying to impress Greenfield with my willingness to treat even a Nazi? Was it conceit and megalomania to think I would be able to treat a hateful bigot successfully? Was it chronic masochism, a recurrent pattern of seeking high risk ventures doomed to failure? Or was it all of the above? I finally decided it was none of the above, but rather it was that the patient and I were the same age and gender and I was attracted to the challenge of relating to him and the opportunity for me to study just how the mind of a Nazi worked.

Heinrich von Himmelhoch proved to be a tall, lean, clean-shaven, blond, stern-faced man, with rimless spectacles and wearing a trim dark suit. He entered my office promptly at our scheduled time and stood stiffly at attention waiting for some direction. I remained seated behind my desk and chose not to rise or greet him. After a few moments of silence he said with a slight clipped German accent, "Where shall I sit?"

I gestured silently at a chair facing my desk.

He stared at me for several minutes and then broke out, "You're a Jew, aren't you?" I stared back at him for a few minutes and then nodded silently.

"I knew it!" he said angrily. "I told that Jew Greenfield that I wanted a Christian therapist and he deliberately assigns me to you."

After a long pause, I said "You are used to getting what you want?"

"Far from it," he replied scornfully. "If I always got what I wanted, I wouldn't be here, would I?"

"Perhaps you still might be here. People frequently find that when they get what they thought they wanted, they don't want it anymore."

"Well, Jew," he sneered, "does that happen with you?"

"Yes. For instance, I thought I wanted to be your therapist, but now that you are here—." I decided to leave the rest of my sentence unsaid.

He flushed and then said loudly, "Well, I want another therapist, and not a Jewish one either."

"I don't think that's possible. I can tell you that when the clinical staff heard about you, I was the only doctor that was willing to take you as a patient. And most of them are not Jewish. I'm afraid that if you wish to continue treatment here, we're both stuck with each other."

"Well," he said sullenly, "if that's the way it is, I guess I have no choice. I'll stay." With that he sat back, put a cigarette into a long cigarette holder, and began smoking, eyeing me silently and waiting for some direction.

After several minutes of silence he said irritably, "Well, what do you want me to talk about?"

"Whatever you want to say or not say is OK with me."

"Well, don't you want to hear why I came here for help?"

"It's not that I want not to hear about that, but neither do I have any wish that you would do that."

He glared at me and suddenly began shouting, "So that's what you're up to—Jewish riddles for me to try to figure out—and you call that 'therapy'? I want a straight answer. Do you or don't you want me to tell you why I came here for help. You're just like my father! Never a straight answer—just a lot of bullshit!" and he suddenly broke out with tears, covering his face with his hands, crying profusely. I silently gave him my box of tissues and waited for several minutes until he dried his eyes.

"Perhaps it might prove helpful if you did tell me what's troubling you."

"Well, It's just that I've been fired again and I'm broke and I'm sure my father will turn me down if I ask him for help." He then launched into a detailed account of his life history while avoiding any eye contact with me. His methodical and chronological presentation of his history not only filled the remainder of his first hour with me, but continued on and on for several weeks.

He had been born in Munich, an only child whose mother died of a brain tumor when he was seven years old. His father had served in the German army during World War II as an engineer and after the war worked for the Volkswagen company. When his father was appointed head of the company's office in New Jersey he took his son, my patient, then fourteen, to live there and married an immigrant German woman. Heinrich disliked his step-mother, was obstreperous with both her and his father and finally was sent to a private boarding school. He then attended college and graduate school, graduating with honors as an electronics engineer. He had several successive jobs assisting with electroencephalography research in medical schools in Massachusetts and later in Connecticut. He lived a lonely life as a research assistant and his jobs never lasted more than three months, since he was invariably fired for insubordination or aggressive quarreling with his superiors.

In his therapy he castigated his former employers, particularly the Jewish ones whom he characterized as sadistic, unappreciative and exploitative "bloodsuckers." I found his arrogant manner and bigoted outbursts offensive and repulsive but kept my contempt to myself, feeling that to express those feelings would be detrimental to his therapy.

He seemed content to continue recounting his life story chronologically session after session without having me respond or comment. I became increasingly uneasy that he was following some preconceived notion as to what a patient was supposed to do in therapy. I feared that by my silence I was reinforcing his stereotyped misconception that probably included an expectation that sooner or later I would eventually use his lengthy narrative to provide curative insights as to his difficulties relating to superiors and others.

Finally, I interrupted his narrative shortly after he began his next session, "Mr. Von Himmelhoch, it appears you've decided that this therapy is a place for you to come and tell me your life history in exquisite detail, and that, somehow, after you've supplied me with your entire autobiography, either I or you or we will use this data to help you or cure you of your problems holding a job. I also notice that you rarely look at me and you speak to me as if you were addressing a tape recorder or a stenographer."

He glared at me and then shouted, "You stupid Jewish quack! Isn't that what Freud said I'm supposed to do here?"

"No."

He jumped to his feet in a rage. "Then why did you let me go on and on all these weeks if that wasn't what you wanted me to do!"

"It is not so that I wanted you *not* to do that. If that is what you want to do, it's OK with me. Nor is it that I want you to stop your anti-Semitic ravings if that is what you want to do here. Nor do I want you to stop your talking at me instead of with me, if that's also what you want to do here."

"Ravings!" he sputtered in a fury, "You're deliberately trying to upset me and I'm getting very angry. Hitler was right! He should have gassed the lot of you!" He paced back and forth, glaring and red-faced and waving his arms about.

I felt glad that my desk was between us and anxiously began wondering what I would do if he actually became assaultive. "Look, Himmelhoch," I said, "you're having a tantrum and behaving like a Nazi lunatic. I can't believe you're really as much of a fan of Hitler or as much of an anti-Semite as you make out to be. You seem too intelligent, and you've apparently sought Freudian therapy for help, even though you know Freud was Jewish. But you've never bothered to check whether I was a Freudian therapist which I am not. However, one thing is certain; namely, that if you behave with your superiors and employers as outrageously as you do with me, it's no wonder that you always get fired."

My long rambling statement seemed to have calmed him down. He slumped down into his chair and again covered his face and began to sob. After a few minutes he dried his tears and said, "My father was a Nazi and hated Jews and never admitted that Hitler was wrong or responsible for the destruction of Germany. I hate being like my father."

The session appeared to be a turning point for my patient. He gradually became more subdued and began sharing with me memories of his father's tyrannical behavior and unrelenting anti-Semitism. He confessed that as he met more Americans in school, college and jobs he began to question his father's bigotry and defense of Hitler and Nazi Germany. But he never risked reaching out for friendship with any of his contemporaries in America and, instead, lived a lonely, bitter, angry life.

He decided to phone his alienated father for financial help, and after telling him that "Jewish doctors" were responsible for getting him fired from his medical school jobs, his father finally relented and agreed to support him financially until he could find another job.

"You are not the first to find that anti-Semitism can be useful financially and politically," I commented.

"Yes," he laughed, "but in my case it was true that my last boss was Jewish and he did fire me."

"I'm sure it was because you were not Jewish and not because you were a pain in the neck to him."

"Careful now, Doctor Jew," he teased, "that was not a proper remark for a psychotherapist to make."

Meanwhile, he reported sending applications for a new job as research assistant to other medical schools outside of Connecticut. Finally, he appeared at his session gleefully waving a letter of acceptance from an out-of-state university for an EEG research appointment. "This is our last meeting, Doctor Jew. I'm off tomorrow and I'm sure you're not sorry to hear that. But I confess I will miss coming here and listening to your stupid Jewish comments."

"Well, Himmelhoch, I'll miss seeing you also. I've always suspected that Nazis were loonies, and I appreciate your convincing me that I was right." We both laughed. He stood up briskly, raised his outstretched arm and shouted, "Heil Hitler!" Turning on his heel, he left laughing.

Months later I received a Christmas card from him. In it he wrote, "Not fired yet. My Jewish boss is stupid enough to like me and my work. Heil Hitler!"

* * * * *

There is a consensus among psychotherapists that the therapist must "like" his patient in order to provide effective psychotherapy. Otherwise, there would be negative, anti-therapeutic, so-called counter-transference behavior by the therapist. I believe this is usually true, but this therapy with a Nazi illustrates that may not always be the case. This patient and I gradually developed a relationship that transcended our mutual antipathy. A rapport based on trust of each other's candor and authenticity did occur and seemed to help him curb his hostile aggressiveness enough to seek and hold his next job working as a research assistant.

11

AN UNEXPECTED OUTCOME

The senior staff sat around the conference table waiting for Dr. Greg Bellows to arrive and begin the weekly meeting. Some sipped coffee and smoked cigarettes as they spoke casually to one another. I was the youngest in the group, having just finished my three year residency in The Yale Department of Psychiatry. Bellows entered and slouched into his chair. He was a big, burly fellow, dark hair, glasses, with a constant expression of bored disdain. Although Chief of Psychiatry in the hospital, he rarely came out of his office where he spent his time writing articles for psychiatric journals.

"Well, guys, what's up?" he said as he filled his coffee cup.

Dr. James Harrison responded quickly, "I've got a serious problem, fellas, and I need your advice." Harrison, a tall, lean, soft-spoken clinician, was chief of one of the open psychiatric wards in the hospital. "There's this patient, Bill Hamper, a paranoid psychopathic enuretic who insists that the Marines ruined his kidneys and bladder, although he was in active military service only a few months. He's furious that he was admitted to Psychiatry instead of Urology. He's been threatening to assault the staff and refuses to talk to any psychiatrists. I decided to transfer him to State Hospital since he's not a service connected veteran and we're not obliged to keep him. But when he learned he was being transferred he came and threatened me. He said that he knew where I lived and that sooner or later he would get out of State Hospital and would then kill me and my family! I'm afraid he means it and I don't trust the staff at State Hospital to keep him there or even warn me if they give him a pass. So that's my problem. What do you think I should do?"

The staff became somber and silent, waiting for Bellows to come up with something. "Look, Jim," Bellows said slowly and deliberately, "I'm sure that if you notify the staff at State Hospital about his threat, they will take appropriate precautions and keep you informed before they think it safe to give him a pass or a discharge."

James shook his head in disagreement. "No, Greg," he said with obvious anxiety, "I can't take that chance. I think we just have to keep him here on our locked ward until he retracts his threat, no matter how long it takes."

Again there was a long and uncomfortable silence in the group. Finally, I blurted out, "Have you considered treating him?" All eyes turned to me, looking as if I had just spoken the unspeakable and deserved to be burned at the stake for heresy.

"Well, Lou," Harrison said angrily, "if you think this psychopath is treatable, why don't you come down to my ward and try it!"

And that's how I became Hamper's therapist. But first I exacted three conditions from Dr. Harrison: (1) that my therapy would be completely confidential. That is, I would not have to share any information about it with him or his staff or enter any but superficial notes in the patient's chart; (2) that I would be totally excused from participating in any administrative decisions about the patient's management, privileges or discipline. I did not want the patient to regard me as part of the ward staff with which he was fighting and, finally; (3) that an aide would be stationed outside the door of whatever room I used for sessions with Hamper in case he became violent.

I must confess that I had a secret motive for volunteering to treat this menacing patient. It had to do with my rivalrous relationship with Dr. Ralph Richards, a colleague of mine in the Yale Department of Psychiatry who had become a star among the junior faculty because of his popular publications about hypnosis research. He claimed to have recovered through hypnosis the earliest memories of patients, going all the way back to infancy. His main "evidence" for the validity of his research was the vividness of detail recalled by his subjects and allegedly confirmed by relatives of the subjects. I envied his popularity and the praise he received from our superiors in the Department. But I was suspicious of his research and doubted the validity of his findings essentially based on the vividness and details of recall. I doubted that an infant's brain would be developed enough to permit the storage of such vivid memories as reported by Richards' subjects. I suspected that his patients were simply complying with his directives to report memories by confabulating memories while under hypnosis. I regarded the alleged confirmation of the recovered memories by relatives as "hearsay evidence," not subject to being proved or unproved.

I speculated that, as an alternative, if a patient under hypnosis were told to project himself into the future and report events in the future, he would report alleged events in the future with as much vividness of detail as reported by Richards' patients in their alleged recollections of their infancy. Such an experiment would then refute the validity of those recollections and expose them as being simply fictitious compliance with hypnotic suggestions. For some time I had been searching unsuccessfully for a subject suitable for such an experiment, and now Mr. Hamper was available.

I reasoned that since he was refusing to accept psychiatric treatment on his ward, he might agree to an offer from an "outside" doctor to treat his alleged traumatic kidney disorder with hypnosis.

Bill Hamper proved to be a short, muscular, red haired, angry, suspicious, 32-year-old man dressed in army fatigue clothes. I introduced myself and explained that although I was a psychiatrist, I was also trained to treat medical conditions with hypnosis, and was willing to try hypnosis for his "kidney problem." He cautiously agreed and we arranged to meet weekly.

I began Hamper's hypnotherapy slowly and carefully, simply trying to get him to relax and trust the hypnotic process. Several sessions passed in which my directives were aimed at promoting a sense of peace and safety in his gradually deepening trance states. Meanwhile his threatening behavior on Dr. Harrison's ward had subsided. He became more cooperative and began to participate in the ward activities program. However, he continued to have nightly bed-wetting and refused to discuss this problem with the staff, telling them he had his own doctor, namely me. He spent much of his time writing angry letters to various agencies of the Federal government demanding compensation for his alleged kidney damage while in the Marines.

In his hypnotherapy Hamper gradually went into deeper and deeper trance states. At the close of each session I would suggest to him that when he came out of his trance he would feel well, relaxed and peaceful; and, indeed, this was the case. Finally, I gave him the hypnotic suggestion that whenever he was with me and I would adjust my tie, he would fall immediately into a deep hypnotic trance state. This eliminated the need for me to take him through a prolonged period of gradual hypnotic induction each time we met. At last I felt ready to do the experiment that would invalidate Dr. Richards' contention that he was able to recover authentic memories from infancy in his hypnotic subjects.

The date was December 1, 1953. Hamper entered my office promptly on schedule and sat down on a chair on the other side of the desk where I was seated.

"Well, Bill, how are things? I asked cheerfully.

"Terrible! I'm not getting any answers to my letters, and I'm sure someone on the staff is keeping them from being mailed. This place is a hell-hole and I'm not going to let those bastards get away with—." I adjusted my tie and in mid-sentence Hamper closed his eyes and slumped down in his chair in a deep hypnotic trance.

"Now, Bill, I want you to listen carefully and do exactly as I tell you to do. When I count from 'A' to 'K' you will wake and you will be in the future one year from today. No matter how much I or anyone else tries to tell you or prove to you that it is not one year from today, you will insist and argue and defend the fact that it is one year from today. You will not remember that I'm telling you to do this but you will remember to do it and you will do it. And now I'm going to count. A * B * C * D * E * F * G * H * I * J * and Kay!"

Hamper opened his eyes, sat up, stretched, took out one of his cigarettes and began to smoke silently.

"Well, Bill, how are things?"

"OK, Doc. This hypnosis makes me feel good each time but it ain't doing much for my kidneys."

"That will take time, Bill, but by the way, do you know what today's date is?"

"Sure, Doc. It's December first." He paused, looked uncomfortable and then added, "1954."

"Oh no, Bill, you mean 1953, don't you?"

"Of course not, it's 1954."

"But Bill, what do you mean it's 1954? It's 1953. Just look at the calendar on the wall."

"What's goin' on, Doc? That's last year's calendar!"

"OK, Bill, if you say so. But tell me, how are things going for you? Where are you living now?"

"In Bridgeport. I live and work there at a hotel, running their elevator." He then went on to describe in great detail his life in Bridgeport, his room in the hotel, his friends, his interest in sports and attendance at sports events.

"When did you leave the hospital, Bill?"

"Did you forget, Doc? It was June first." He began to appear agitated and so I adjusted my tie and once again Hamper sank into a deep trance.

"Bill, I'm going to count from one to ten and you will then awake. You will forget everything that happened during your trance this afternoon. But in future hypnosis sessions with me you will remember what happened this afternoon whenever I tell you to remember. And you will return to the future you told me about this afternoon if I ask you to. I will now count from one to ten and you will awake and will feel fine, rested and cheerful." Hamper left the session in a cheerful mood, claiming no memory of what had transpired.

The hypnotherapy continued week after week with Hamper reporting many stories about his alleged future life in Bridgeport. Although his general ward behavior had improved, his complaints about his bed-wetting became more shrill, strident and threatening. I decided to interrupt my project of eliciting his stories about his life in the future and concentrate on using hypnosis to stop his enuresis.

Research on hypnotherapy had established that the removal of patients' symptoms by means of directive hypnotic suggestions rarely lasted more than a few days. However, Milton Erikson, M.D., "the father of American hypnosis," had devised a strategy of symptom substitution for patients with disabling hysterical symptoms (Erikson, 1967). That is, he used hypnotic suggestion to get patients to exchange their disabling symptom for a non-disabling symptom that would still gratify the patient's underlying psychological or unconscious motive and need that originally led to the hysterical disabling symptom.

It occurred to me that if I could induce the symptom of a moderately painful knee in Hamper, he might give up his bed-wetting. He could then still claim that his knee had been injured during his brief military career in the Marines and he could continue to harass the government for compensation as a service-connected injured veteran. But at least he would no longer be socially disabled and would be able to live in his community without the stigma and rejection caused by his enuresis.

We were well into March of 1954 when I began trying hypnotic suggestion to "cure" his enuresis by directing him to have an arthritic knee instead.

"Bill, I greeted, "how are you today?"

"Look, Doc," he said angrily, "it's been months now and this hypno treatment just ain't working and I'm beginning to get pissed off at you!" I silently noted the irony of his rhetoric about being "pissed off" as I adjusted my tie and Hamper obediently slipped into a deep trance.

"Now, Bill, I'm going to count from 'A' to 'K' and when I reach 'K' you will wake and feel great, rested and cheerful. But tonight you will not wet your bed, and if you have to urinate, you will wake up and go to the bathroom and urinate there. And you will do this every night until we meet again next week. You will not remember my telling you this but you will remember to not wet your bed and to go to the bathroom if you have to urinate." I then counted him to wakefulness and after some small talk about his grievances with the ward staff, we ended the session.

One week later he bounded into the room and greeted me excitedly. "Hey, Doc!" he exclaimed, "I think it's beginning to work. All week after I fell asleep I heard your voice yelling in the middle of the night, 'Bill! Get up and go to the bathroom!' And I got up and went to the bathroom and I haven't peed in bed all week!"

I interrupted his gleeful state by adjusting my tie, once again sending him deep into his hypnotic trance. "Bill," I said sternly, "you will continue to not wet your bed and instead go to the bathroom. But you will begin to notice pain in your right knee. You will complain to the ward staff about it but nothing they do or try or medicate will relieve the pain. The pain will not be severe and will not keep you awake. When I count from 'A' to 'K' you will wake and feel good and not remember that I told you about going to the bathroom or developing some pain in your right knee, but you will do both things."

As the weeks went by Hamper continued to comply with my weekly hypnotic suggestions that he avoid wetting his bed and instead complain about a painful right knee. Despite negative examinations and tests of his knee he insisted that his knee must have been injured while he was in the Marines. He demanded and was given a cane and limped around the hospital while scorning the inability of the medical staff to "fix" his knee.

Meanwhile, I was preparing my notes and data about his confabulated projection into the future and anticipating the impact my report would have on the faculty and my rival, Dr. Richards. My scheme was dashed by the events that occurred May 15, 1954.

"Doc," Hamper began the session, "let's skip the hypno today. I've been thinking I've been in this hell-hole long enough. I called my old boss at the hotel in Bridgeport where I worked as a bell-boy 'til he fired me because of my peeing in bed there. I told him you fixed my kidneys so I don't pee in bed anymore and he's offered me a job running his elevator starting June first. Room and board and four bucks an hour ain't bad, at least 'til I win my law suit against those bastards in Washington. Doc—what's the matter? You don't look so good. Are you sick or something?"

Indeed, I was flabbergasted—speechless—amazed! How could this be? How could he be telling me now that he was going to do what he had said he had already done when he was hypnotically projected one year into the future? And what about the job, the elevator, living in Bridgeport and leaving the hospital June first?

I stood up and congratulated Hamper, shook his hand and offered to see him as an out-patient if he wanted to continue his treatment with me. He said he would think about it and left my office, using his cane as he limped away.

Hamper signed out of the hospital June first and took the elevator job and went to live in Bridgeport, just as he had said he did in his trance six months before. I decided that my plan to present my experiment with him to the Yale faculty in order to refute Dr. Richards' hypnosis research was no longer feasible in view of the strange and inexplicable outcome.

Hamper did call me for an appointment three months later. It turned out that all he wanted was to tell me he was getting married and had dropped his law suit against the government. He still used his cane because of the "knee injury" he claimed he had received while in military service.

*   *   *   *   *

Hypnosis to this day is still not well understood or scientifically studied. Clinical hypnotists always appear to me to be enjoying their seemingly magical power over their subjects' minds. And after submitting to hypnosis the hypnosands always appear to be somewhat dismayed and embarrassed that they so readily surrendered their autonomy. I look back on my experiment with Hamper over forty years ago with some guilt and shame that I gave so much priority to research interests and rivalry with Dr. Richards rather than focussing primarily on the patient's need for treatment for his conversion hysteria and his psychopathy.

Even to suggest that hypnosis had made it possible for my patient to predict the future accurately and in vivid detail was totally unacceptable to me, both then and now. To speculate that he had planned the outcome six months before and had presented his plan while under the throes of a post-hypnotic suggestion also seemed too farfetched to be considered seriously. The only explanation acceptable to me is that there was coincidence between his description while in a trance and the actual events that occurred six months later. Coincidences frequently lend themselves to fallacious claims that something magical has happened.

I discontinued using hypnotherapy for therapy or research after a few years because I increasingly felt it was a procedure that reinforced patients' dependency and, therefore, was antithetical to effective psychotherapy.

12

THE HIGH-PROFILE PATIENT

"You know, Doctor, I was thirty-five years old when I married Jack, and then two years later he died. And there I was, six months pregnant, no family, few friends, no job, living alone in our little house, mourning his death and drinking every day and all day.

"Jack and I had a little ritual. He'd come home from teaching at the hospital about 5:30 every afternoon and I would have two martinis prepared and we would sit in our den and sip our drinks and tell each other about our day. After he died I continued to do the same thing every afternoon at 5:30. I'd sip my martini and talk to him and feel he was there with me, listening to me telling him about my day. Only difference was that after I finished my martini I drank his too. And pretty soon I was drinking vodka all day long. 'Drowning my sorrow in booze,' I'm sure you're thinking. But I guess that is what I was doing.

"Then I finally had my baby, Susan. She's three years old now, but I've continued my daily tippling, and yesterday I picked up the frying pan I was cooking with and didn't feel how hot the handle was until it burned my hand badly. So I called 911 and they brought me here to the hospital and admitted me to Surgery for my hand. After a day or so of not having anything to drink in the hospital I guess I got the D.T.s and began seeing cats all around me and saw cats getting killed by jumping out of the window. I started screaming for help and they transferred me here to Psychiatry, and that's my story."

Florence Williams was my patient on the University Hospital Psychiatric Ward where I was Chief Resident. Out of respect for her status as widow of a recently deceased popular professor, my chief had asked me to be her therapist rather than assign her to one of the junior residents. I met with her daily as she went through alcohol detoxification.

She was a gentle, dignified, soft-spoken, forty-year-old, attractive woman with a history of being the only child of parents who owned a dairy farm in Vermont. A shy, studious student, she had avoided socializing and read voraciously. She rarely dated, graduated from college with honors and earned a Ph.D. in Sociology. After joining the faculty at Yale, she avoided involvements with suitors, indulged her interests in painting and finally at age thirty-five she met and, after a brief courtship, married Dr. Jack Williams, a Yale Professor of Surgery, also thirty-five. In her second year of marriage she became pregnant but midway in her pregnancy Jack became ill with kidney disease and died suddenly of kidney failure and uremia.

Florence had presented her history in a straightforward, unembellished manner and seemed to be over her craving for alcohol. "I think you're ready to leave the hospital, Florence," I said after four weeks, "but I strongly recommend that you see someone to continue your psychotherapy after you leave. I'll be glad to make arrangements for you to see one of our senior attending psychiatrists."

"Why can't I see you? I heard from other patients here that you have an evening private practice. What's the problem? Don't you want me as a patient anymore?" Her eyes teared and her voice trembled as she made her plaintive plea.

I was taken aback by her request and replied, "Well, we don't usually refer patients who are hospitalized here to ourselves, but I'll check with my chief. If he approves I'll be glad to see you privately."

My chief, Dr. Thomas Lambert, was a tall, lean, fiftyish academic, famous for his research on drug addiction. "Lou, let me give you some advice," he said, "Florence Williams is a high-profile patient and a chronic alcoholic. Her prognosis is poor and it's unlikely you're going to be able to do much for her. You're just starting out in private practice and your failure with her will be known all over the university community. It's too risky for you. Better refer her to one of our older attending psychiatrists."

I thanked him but left his office feeling perturbed and disappointed. What was my chief saying? Play it safe and treat only low risk patients? Since when had that become part of the Hippocratic Oath? I decided to reject his advice and went directly to the ward, sought out Florence and gave her an appointment for therapy with me following her discharge.

Within a few weeks I was regretting not having taken my chief's advice. Florence was home and drinking again, showing up at my office for therapy clearly inebriated.

She refused my suggestion that she be readmitted to the hospital and also my appeal that she join Alcoholics Anonymous. I also worried about her driving to and from the office while under the influence of alcohol. She had hired a maid to help care for her daughter, but I still was concerned about the child's welfare being raised by an alcoholic mother.

"Florence," I finally confessed, "I've become too worried and distracted about your drinking to be of much help to you as a psychotherapist. I'm afraid I have to stop your therapy with me and insist that you either go back to the hospital or else continue therapy with someone else." She began to weep and my own sense of guilt and frustration escalated. After several minutes of painful silence I relented and said, "Florence, I didn't mean what I just said and perhaps I've been over-reacting. It's your life and you have the right to decide whether to drink or not to drink. I should not make sobriety a condition for my being your therapist. I promise to continue seeing you for therapy, drunk or sober, for as long as you want and as long as it is helpful to you."

"Thank you," she said as she dried her eyes and the session ended. The following week she appeared, clearly sober, and carrying a large cardboard box containing a dozen bottles of vodka. "I didn't have the heart to throw away all these bottles of excellent vodka," she said. "I'd like you to have them." I took the bottles without comment. That session seemed to be a turning point for Florence. Her commitment to abstinence and sobriety proved resolute. With minimal symptoms of withdrawal she devoted herself to the care of her child and to her painting.

The months seemed to pass quickly as she cheerfully filled her therapy hours with reports, reminiscences and commentaries on the daily news. I became increasingly uneasy about the plateau quality of the therapy and the absence of any sign of movement in her condition. Finally I commented, "Florence, you seem to have an attitude toward your therapy that even though the seasons may come and go, and Susan may grow older and taller and your flower garden may blossom and then wither, but just like that famous song from *Showboat*, 'Ole Man River—he just keeps rolling along,' this therapy just keeps rolling along without end or purpose."

She became silent and downcast. "You mean maybe it's time for me to stop?"

"Well, it is puzzling to me why you continue. You don't present any pressing problems and nothing significant has happened in your therapy for months."

She responded sheepishly, "I keep coming because you're the only friend I have and I enjoy our sessions together."

"Well, Florence, I am your friend and I'm glad you enjoy your therapy, but what does it mean that you have but one friend and that one is your therapist? I think the reason may be that you've put the 'no vacancy' sign out, so to speak. I think you may have turned away from the many people out there who knew you and your husband and who would be delighted to be your friend and share your interests in painting, social issues and daughter rearing."

Florence smiled and agreed, "I guess I've always been a loner and avoided social activity. But for Susan's sake, if not for my own, I agree with you that I should become more active in the community. And I know that there are people around whom I do like and who have children who would like to play with Susan." Later she informed me that she had joined a local art society and also a faculty wives group and was enjoying meeting new friends and colleagues. Finally, she announced her decision to stop her therapy.

In the years that followed I met her at various social occasions. After her grown daughter had married, Florence returned to teaching and also enjoyed her grandchildren with no recurrence of alcoholism.

*　*　*　*　*

There are few more challenging disorders facing psychotherapists than substance abuse disorders, particularly alcoholism. The claim of advocates of Alcoholics Anonymous that their successes are much greater than those achieved by psychotherapists is probably true. The issue is motivation and how to overcome the patient's compelling urge to seek the comfort and relief from misery provided by the potent addicting substance. Prognosis is better if the alcoholism is triggered by a catastrophic event as in this case. My willingness to replace her lost husband's affection with my own unconditional acceptance ("I promise to continue seeing you for therapy, drunk or sober . . .") appeared to be a turning point in this therapy, lifting the intensity of her motivation enough so as to overcome the intensity of her compulsion to drink.

However, even that pledge may not have served as a turning point were it not for the relationship of communicative-intimacy gradually established over the previous many weeks of therapy. Moreover, it is not just finding the "right" words or saying what the patient wants to hear. If a therapist is genuinely committed to his patient (i.e., to providing a curative therapeutic experience), this fact will sooner or later become apparent and be a central factor in fostering the patient's self-esteem and creative behavior, leading to a healthier, more mature and independent life style.

13

GOTCHA!

This therapy started out on an old familiar theme: Helen was married to Menelaus but loved Paris; Guinevere was married to Arthur but loved Lancelot; Catherine was married to Edgar but loved Heathcliff; and my patient, Virginia Jones, was married to Richard but loved Tony. She wept frequently during the hours she spent talking about her sad story. She had been in love with Tony since childhood. Their families were friends and lived in the same neighborhood in New Haven. Her father was a schoolteacher and Tony's father owned the neighborhood grocery store. Tony and Virginia were classmates and studied together in their homes. He was an athlete and on the high school wrestling team. She played flute in the school orchestra. In high school they became secret lovers, careful to avoid pregnancy. After graduation she left home to go to college at her state university and majored in music. Tony stayed home to work in the family store and help his ailing father.

At college Virginia's statuesque beauty, intelligence and dignified demeanor attracted scores of suitors. Her commitment of loyalty and fidelity to Tony gradually weakened under the onslaught of her popularity and she finally became engaged to Richard, a varsity football star, psychology major and son of a wealthy corporate executive. Tony received a "Dear Tony" letter and sadly wished her well.

Virginia and Richard were married the summer after their graduation and when they returned from their Bermuda honeymoon they rented a small apartment in New Haven. He had been active in the Reserve Officer Training Corps while at college and was obligated now to serve on active duty in the Army. The country was in the throes of the Vietnam War and Richard was sent to Fort Dix in Alabama for basic training for combat duty.

Virginia remained in New Haven and worked as a school music teacher. She felt lonely despite frequent phone calls from her absent husband. While visiting her parents in her old neighborhood she was surprised to see Tony arrive to deliver the groceries they had ordered. It was re-love at first sight and within a few days they renewed their old secret love affair, careful not to be discovered by their parents. Tony pleaded with her to divorce Richard and marry him. But Virginia still cared for Richard and did not want to hurt him. Also Richard's wealth provided her with a standard of living that Tony would not be able to match.

She became increasingly guilt-ridden over her infidelity to Richard and her procrastination with Tony and soon developed symptoms of anxiety, tension headaches, insomnia and depression. She felt it increasingly difficult to think clearly or make a decision about Tony or Richard and finally decided to seek psychiatric help. Her family physician referred her to me.

"It must be very sad to love someone and not be able to live with that person," I said as she sobbed in my office. "But I notice that for every reason you raise for ending your marriage with Richard, you seem to come up with an equally weighty reason for not. It's as if you are deliberately avoiding a decision by making sure that all the cons equal all the pros."

"No," she objected, "that's not true. The reasons for and against are really equal and I'm not pretending it's that way." Feeling it would be too stressful for her if I challenged her denial, I remained silent. After several minutes went by while she sulked silently, she finally broke out, "Well, why do you think I'm doing that?"

"There are several possibilities. One is that since it's a painful decision to make, people procrastinate with the hope that something will happen either to make the decision for them or to make the decision unnecessary. Another is that they may hope that someone who is familiar with their dilemma will take pity on their suffering and make the decision for them. And then there are some who become very anxious and even panicky if they have to make an important decision because of a lifelong feeling that they are not qualified or authorized to be an independent and autonomous person."

Virginia laughed and said, "I think 'all the above' would apply to me. But, something is happening that may change things. Richard phoned and has a week's leave and he's coming home next week. He knows I'm seeing you but thinks it's because of my anxiety and depression over being alone these past months. He says he wants to come with me to see you. Is that OK with you?"

"It's OK with me."

When Virginia and her husband appeared it was clear that they were in crisis. Richard was obviously in a rage, red-faced, fists clenched, avoiding touching or looking at Virginia and instead glaring angrily at me. He was tall, robust, muscular and dressed in his second lieutenant's army uniform. Virginia was pale, downcast and staring at the floor. They silently seated themselves and Richard then reached into his jacket and pulled out an envelope and thrust it at me. "Read that, Doctor!" he snarled.

"Virginia," I said, "do you want me to read this?" She nodded and began to sob. I slowly removed the contents of the envelope. They consisted of a printed four-page questionnaire with a cover letter from the American Psychological Association addressed to Mrs. Richard Jones stating that a questionnaire was being sent to all husbands and wives in the country who had married in the past year. The letter assured the reader that the questionnaire would take only fifteen minutes to fill out and would be completely confidential, unsigned and unidentified and used only for statistical research on the status and nature of marriage in the United States. There were about fifty questions relating to age, gender, race, class, education, religion, job history, courtship, sexual history, sexual practices, pregnancies and fidelity since getting married plus questions about health and medical or psychiatric treatment.

The questionnaire had been completely filled out by some unnamed person. "So what's all this about, Richard?" I asked.

"Don't you see?" he shouted. "That's Virginia's confession that she's been fucking someone else! And she won't tell me who it is!"

"But what makes you think this is Virginia's questionnaire?"

"Because it's the only questionnaire there is, you fool; because I made the whole thing up and had it printed and mailed to her with a self-addressed return envelope to a post office box in order to find out if she was faithful or not, and she checked the God-damned infidelity question!" And then he began to weep along with Virginia.

I sat there dumbfounded, awestruck by this fantastic deception. I watched silently as Virginia reached out to console her distraught husband. He shoved her hand away violently, leaped to his feet and shouted, "Damn it, Virginia, I gotcha red-handed! Who is he? What's his name? I have a right to know!"

Fearing violence I decided to resort to a strategy I use at times when I'm with a patient who seems to be having an escalating rage and is threatening violence; namely, to begin a calm, protracted sort of filibuster and make a long rambling statement, continuing until the patient is distracted from his fury and settles down. "Richard, I can understand your anger and your pain and your impulse to strike out and punish Virginia, but you must consider that there may be aspects of the situation that you don't yet know about that might make you see things differently than you do now and. . . ." On and on I droned for about five minutes while Richard slumped down on his chair, covered his face and waited impatiently for me to finish my lengthy statement. Finally, he stood up and interrupted, "Doctor, I've had enough of your bullshit!" Then turning to Virginia he said sternly, "And I've had it with you too, Virginia, and I'm going back to my base and I'm going to get a divorce, and I'm going to take you off of my health insurance too, so you're going to have to pay your quack doctor-shrink yourself." Turning on his heel, he stomped off.

Virginia and I stared at each other, dazzled by his bombastic departure. Then we both broke out laughing.

"Free at last," she cried, "It looks like Richard has solved my problem. But how am I going to pay you if he drops me from his insurance?"

"Don't worry, Virginia." I said, "I've been in the Army and know that a soldier cannot stop his insurance from covering his spouse's medical bills once she has started her treatment."

Her therapy continued for several months taking her through her divorce, dealing with her disappointed parents, and living with Tony while they waited for her divorce to clear the way to their own marriage.

* * * * *

The outcome of this therapy was clearly determined by forces outside the control or influence of the therapy; namely, the psychopathic craftiness and duplicity of the patient's husband which led to the bizarre questionnaire entrapment of his wife which then led to the divorce she had wanted but was too indecisive to initiate herself. The therapy was supportive and helped her be more decisive and take advantage of her second chance at a happy marriage.

An unanswered question is how to account for her husband's suspicions about her. Is there some basic, ubiquitous male paranoia about women's fidelity related to males' long history of attempts to dominate and control females; i.e., the use of "chastity belts" for wives during the Middle Ages and also the use of eunuchs to guard Arabian harems? Or had there been some subtle change in Virginia's phone conversations or letters that aroused Richard's suspicions? His angry, hasty departure prevented the question from being asked or answered.

14

A FATAL SUCCESS

Robert Thompson was depressed, profoundly so, and with good reason. His brief marriage of two years was on the rocks, and, as the old saying goes, the rocks were in his marital bed. He was a prominent clinical psychologist, busy in his private practice, fortyish, lean, handsome, intense, intelligent and articulate. We were old friends and his phone call asking for an appointment came as a surprise to me.

"Lou," he explained in his first therapy hour, "I can't take it any more. Wendy is impossible and now she wants a divorce!" He described his predicament. He had married Wendy, a psychiatric social worker, after a brief courtship. It was his first marriage, her second, and there was Brad, her teenage son from her previous marriage. She had initiated the divorce from her alcoholic and abusive former husband over the objections of Brad who had enjoyed a close relationship with his father and blamed her for both his father's drinking and the divorce. Brad was undisciplined, openly hostile to Robert and able to intimidate his mother whenever she tried to discipline him. He was rude, vulgar and abusive to her, but whenever Robert tried to intervene on her behalf, Wendy would side with Brad and order Robert to "stay out of it."

Their home situation went from bad to worse, with Robert criticizing Wendy for her passivity and leniency with Brad; Brad defiant and insulting, and Wendy increasingly rejecting Robert's sexual advances at night. When, finally, Robert responded to Brad's insolence by slapping him, Wendy became furious, refused to sleep with him and finally demanded that he move out. He did move to a motel, became increasingly depressed and finally called me for help. We arranged for weekly psychotherapy. He refused my offer to prescribe antidepressant medication.

In his therapy hours Robert ventilated his anger and frustration toward Wendy and Brad and appeared content to have me simply listen to his catharsis without responding. He frequently used one of the foam rubber Bataka bats I have in the office to help patients release their suppressed anger. He would pound the pillows of my couch with the bat as he cursed Brad and Wendy.

One day he began his hour by reporting a dream, "I was walking alone on a deserted beach when suddenly I felt I had to go to a bathroom to have a bowel movement. I came to a beach toilet area but when I entered I found all the toilet bowls were covered with fine mesh wire. I panicked and woke up in a cold sweat." He stared at me expectantly. "What do you think it means, Lou?"

"As you know very well, Bob, you are the author of your own dreams."

"But I just draw a blank on that. What do you think I'm trying to tell myself?"

"Well, my association to your dream is that you seem to use your therapy and my ear as a kind of toilet, a place where you can come and dump all your feelings with the hope that purging your self of all your painful feelings will solve your dilemma as to what to do about Wendy and Brad. But like the toilet that doesn't work, you've become aware that catharsis alone does not work and that you still have to make some sort of decision and take some sort of action about your marriage and that seems to frighten you."

After a long silence Bob became quite agitated. His depressed mood suddenly seemed to lift and he shouted excitedly, "Of course you're right! I've been a passive jerk to let them push me around and I'm not going to take it any more!" To my dismay he leaped up and left my office hurriedly, calling out as he left, "I'll see you next week, Lou."

I became anxious and worried about his impulsive flight and his strange response, seemingly unconnected to anything I had said. I feared that my remarks might have inadvertently set off a manic reaction, a phenomenon not uncommon in the treatment of depressed people who have the latent potential of cycling between depression and mania, a so-called manic-depressive or bipolar mood disorder.

My fears were confirmed the next day when I received a call from a local state mental hospital psychiatrist telling me that when Bob returned to his home from my office he had physically assaulted his wife and stepson. Although not seriously injured, they were able to call the police who came to their rescue, arrested Bob, and then had him admitted involuntarily to the hospital.

Bob was a patient there for a month on a locked ward, phoning me repeatedly, protesting his incarceration and refusing medications. When I finally refused to take his calls, he wrote to me demanding that I get him out of the hospital. I wrote back urging him to submit to the doctor's treatment in order to get released and apparently he decided to take my advice. He then submitted passively to the hospital treatment plan which included Lithium and other antipsychotic medications and was finally discharged. However, immediately after leaving the hospital he discontinued taking his medication and called to make an appointment to see me.

When we met, it was apparent that Robert was now in the throes of a manic state. He boisterously proclaimed that he had not returned to me to continue his own psychotherapy, but, rather, to treat me for my neurosis! He invoked a previous article written by my own late therapist, Hellmuth Kaiser, that made the point that effective psychotherapy required an egalitarian relationship of communicative-intimacy between therapist and patient, and that even a patient could treat his therapist if the patient had that kind of relationship with the therapist (Kaiser, 1962).

Robert neglected to include in his reference to that article that the relationship and communication described were completely nondirective and nonauthoritarian. Instead he loudly began to confront me with a list of my mannerisms, behavioral styles, wimpiness and other alleged character flaws and demanded that I immediately cease and desist from indulging in them. He did this while pacing around the office, pointing and gesturing, red-faced and agitated. This harangue continued throughout the hour. I thanked him for his concern and tried to persuade him to continue to take his antimanic medication. He took umbrage at this and stormed out the door.

I never saw Robert alive again. I learned over the next few months that he had divorced his wife, was living with another woman and had returned to his private practice despite his manic state of mind. Finally, the sad news arrived that a patient of his had shot and killed him.

* * * * *

Manic-depression or bipolar mood disorder responds fairly well to a combination of antidepressant, antimanic and antipsychotic medication plus psychotherapy. There is the danger, illustrated in this case, that once the depression is lifted the patient is at risk of shifting into a manic phase. One way to prevent this, if there is a history of previous manic episodes, is to start the patient on antimanic medication while he is still depressed. With this patient there was no such history. He had presented only with depression, and the outburst of manic behavior was sudden and unpredictable. Also, he had refused medication even for his depression. Although one might say that psychotherapy was successful in freeing him from depression, an apparent and unpredicted consequence was the emergence of a latent mania which may have contributed to his untimely death.

All clinicians learn quickly that not all therapies are successful or lead to happy gratifying outcomes. Was there anything I might have done differently? With hindsight I would have made even more effort to contact him by phoning or writing after he left me and therapy and would have tried harder to persuade him to take his Lithium medication and continue his psychotherapy, either with me or some other therapist. But there are no "if only"s in real life—only regrets.

The turning point in this case seems to have been when I interpreted his dream. He seized on my speculation and used it to initiate his manic state. I believe he equated the blocked toilet in his dream with his own fearfully suppressed angry aggression against his wife and stepson. When I stated my thought that his dream reflected the failure of passive catharsis in his therapy to resolve his domestic crisis he may have assumed incorrectly that I was encouraging more decisive action, including the perverse notion that what he needed to do was to become more assertive, aggressive and even violent.

His basic fear of his own anger and potential violence intensified. Rather than face that fear and deal with it in therapy he fled into manic, aggressive and violent behavior. The manic behavior may even have been an important factor in his own patient's violent murderous behavior against him. A sad loss of a gifted, dedicated psychologist, psychotherapist and friend.

Accepting a close friend into therapy should be avoided if possible. However, if the friend persists, caution should be explicitly expressed; namely, that the therapy may strain the relationship of friendship and may even end it. If the friend still persists, the therapist must make an inner commitment to give priority to the needs of the therapy.

I was devastated by the tragic death of my friend.

15

THE DANCE

"My husband is a good man and I love him, but not the way I want to love someone. And he loves me, but not the way I want to be loved," Janice Karlson spoke in my office downcast, avoiding eye contact, twisting her handkerchief and near tears.

She was forty-two years old, married to an engineer; two daughters, one age twenty-one, the other nineteen. She was a social worker at a local Family Service agency and was referred to me by another social worker who had been a former patient of mine. On the phone Janice reported that she was depressed and having marital problems and wanted to talk to someone about them.

In the course of her therapy she reported that she had been born in upstate Wisconsin. Her parents were Danish dairy farmers; she was the youngest of four children, but the only one to go to college where she met and subsequently married her husband, Peter, also of Danish descent. They both attended graduate school in Connecticut and found jobs in New Haven afterwards.

"My oldest daughter, Roberta, is studying nursing in Boston but my youngest daughter, Lillian, began behaving strangely in her freshman year at the University of Connecticut and was sent home. She had been found in December wandering about the campus, barefoot, no warm clothes, singing to herself and disoriented. They diagnosed schizophrenia and we brought her home. Since then she has been living with us and seeing her psychiatrist, Dr. Sherman, for the past year. He has her on Prolixin and sees her briefly once a month for medication monitoring. I thought she should have psychotherapy but both Peter and Dr. Sherman disagreed and argued that schizophrenia is a medical brain disorder and psychotherapy is not indicated and would do no good. I'm very annoyed with both of them about this."

"Janice," I said, "you know there's no law against a mother treating her own daughter." She seemed startled by my comment.

"What are you suggesting, Doctor? That I do psychotherapy with my own daughter?"

"And why not. You are a trained social worker. Perhaps if you related to your daughter as if she were a nineteen-year-old with an intact brain who is troubled by all the sorts of things that trouble teenagers, she might respond in a more rational way. You may recall that Ophelia behaved strangely after Hamlet jilted her and, as far as I know, no one has labeled her schizophrenic."

Janice seemed to perk up after this exchange and for several weeks focused on her unhappiness with Peter, her husband. "He's a cold fish," she complained, "He takes no initiative with me. I have to start our conversations, arrange our social life, invite him for sex, plan our vacations. He's affable but totally unromantic. The truth is I'm bored with him and our marriage."

"Let's see if I understand," I said, "Your problem in your marriage is that your husband will do anything you ask him to do, but will not do anything unless you ask him to do it?" She stared at me quizzically.

"Are you making fun of me, Doctor?"

"You're very perceptive, Janice, and I guess I was being a bit sarcastic and I apologize. But, frankly, having a passive and compliant husband may make your marriage boring, but it hardly qualifies as a failed marriage. I believe George Bernard Shaw is alleged to have said that the secret of a successful marriage is that the spouses do not dislike one another."

"I'm sorry, Doctor Fierman, but I don't find my situation funny at all and I resent your not taking me more seriously. You've been a great help to me in my relationship with my daughter, but no help at all with my husband, and I'm on the verge of quitting with you."

"Perhaps if you were as confronting with your husband as you are with me," I responded, "it might motivate him to change for the better." Janice did not quit and the therapy moved on with her becoming more and more despondent and pessimistic about her marriage.

"If Peter is so compliant why don't you tell him to get some psychotherapy himself?" I said. Janice agreed but later reported that Peter had quit after seeing another psychiatrist a few times.

"He says there's nothing wrong with him and the problem is with me and I'm afraid he's right. I'm afraid I just don't love him anymore." She began sobbing as I sat in silence, feeling impotent and ineffectual.

Finally I commented, "Janice, you've made the point that you are very unhappy with your marriage, but for some reason you never mention divorce as an option."

After a long pause she dried her eyes and with head bowed, spoke softly, "I have a confession to make, Doctor. Early in our marriage, after my first child was born, I realized I had made a big mistake marrying Peter. A fellow social worker, new to the agency, became attracted to me, although he too was married, and, finally, we had a brief affair. I'm sure he was the father of my second child, Lillian, although Peter assumes she is his daughter. I still feel guilty about the whole thing and wonder whether my unhappiness and even Lillian's illness may not be some sort of punishment. Maybe I don't have the right to divorce Peter after all I've done to him."

"I don't see how continuing to live with Peter, feeling as you do about him and your marriage, is doing him a service. But I can understand your reluctance to cause him more grief by divorcing him."

Our weekly sessions continued but her therapy seemed to be at an impasse, with her seeming unable to decide whether to stay and make the best of the situation or whether to end the marriage once and for all. To my surprise she ended a session by reporting, "Doctor, I haven't told you yet, but I have been attending a dance class for months. I wanted to be a ballet dancer when I was a child but my parents couldn't afford the classes. I find it very relaxing and it helps me forget my miseries. It's a class for developing expressive dancing and I think it's helping me decide what to do about my marriage. I'd like to try an experiment and do my dance here next time. I think maybe it will help you help me."

"Wow!" I said, having no previous experience in my training or in my practice for dealing with such a request, "Sure, why not, if that's what you would like to do."

The following week Janice appeared wearing a long coat. Without a word she began rearranging the furniture so as to have a large clear area in the center of the office. She placed a chair for me in a corner and then took off her coat and her shoes. She was wearing a knee-length, simple, sheath-like, plain, loose, sleeveless dress. Draped about her shoulders was a long, voluminous, semi-transparent, gossamer, flimsy, shawl-like, dusky colored, patterned cloth. She unpinned her hair which she usually wore coiled high on her head, allowing it to fall to her shoulders. My office is usually dimly lit and as she stood silently in the center of its small Persian rug she appeared statuesque, like some exotic princess out of an Arabian Nights storybook. Slowly lifting her arms she began to sway and turn and bend, her movements synchronous with some inner silent rhythm. As she pirouetted around, first on one foot and then the other, eyes closed, hair swirling, arms twisting, the pace of movements escalated. The gossamer shawl wound and unwound around her as she whirled about, first in one direction and then the reverse. Her arms and legs began thrusting out as she shook back and forth as if to rid herself of some clinging force. Faster and faster she twirled until with a great spring upward she collapsed to the floor, curled in a fetal position, face down, shuddering and moaning.

The entire dance had lasted about ten minutes. I had watched spellbound, captivated by the intensity and emotionality of the non-verbal plea that seemed to permeate her every movement. Her dance seemed to shout at me, "I want to be free!"

Janice slowly sat up, regained her composure and returned to her chair, staring intently at me. After a long silence she stated firmly, "I want a divorce."

"Yes, I know."

This strange session seemed to have resolved her dilemma as to what she should do. Within a few weeks

Janice confronted her husband and they agreed to an amicable divorce. She resigned from her job and made arrangements to return to her childhood home in Wisconsin with her daughter, now much improved psychologically, thanks in part to her daily scheduled conversations with her mother.

In her final session we shared thoughts about her dance. "I felt like I was a bird," she explained, "trying to escape from a cage that was open but I was being blown back by a fierce wind."

"To me you looked like an Arabian princess on a magic carpet trying to fly to freedom but struggling to overcome some kind of magic force trying to pull you back."

We both laughed and hugged farewell as she left the office.

* * * * *

Patients frequently use psychotherapy to help them make difficult life-changing decisions. Their innate basic dependency will be reinforced if the therapist is too active in trying to influence them to make a decision the therapist thinks best for them. Patients are best served by a therapist who encourages and supports them to arrive at their own decisions their own way. He may confront such patients with their procrastination, rationalizations and dependency, but should not go beyond this by recommending his own preference. In the case of Janice, I was actually inclined to prefer that she should become reconciled with her husband, but, fortunately, I abstained, allowing the patient to find her own path through the unusual means of listening to her own deepest feelings as they emerged in her expressive dancing.

16

BETTER LATE
THAN NEVER

Donald and Mary Statler stood up quickly when I entered the waiting room to greet them. They were both white faced, holding hands tightly and looking anguished. "I'm Dr. Fierman," I said, "Please come in."

They entered my office cautiously and then stood still, clearly waiting for me to direct them. I sat down on my recliner and waited silently. "Where shall we sit?" he finally asked.

"Anywhere you please," I answered. She chose the couch while he sat on the recliner opposite mine. "Mr. Statler, when your family doctor, Dr. Levine, phoned and asked me to see the two of you he told me that you are a high school principal, and that you, Mrs. Statler, are a music teacher, and that he had advised marital counseling for the two of you. And that's all I know about you."

After a few minutes of silence during which each seemed to be waiting for the other to begin, Mary spoke up, "The problem is that Don wants a divorce. We've just celebrated our twenty-fifth anniversary and then he tells me he wants a divorce. He says he wants his freedom." She then burst into tears. Don handed her his handkerchief. After drying her eyes she continued, "I told him I would agree to a divorce only if he would agree first to a trial period of marriage counseling. He did and I called Dr. Levine who recommended you and arranged the appointment."

Mary was forty-eight; Don fifty-two. She was about five-and-a-half feet tall; he was about six feet. She had graying straight brunette hair which she wore cut short; he had a slightly receding hairline and also graying brunette hair. She wore no makeup or jewelry and was dressed neatly and primly in a plain patterned dress and knit sweater. He wore a plaid jacket, starched shirt, bright red striped tie and neatly pressed dark trousers. They reminded me of the cardinals in my back yard, the male all red and feisty and the female, dusky brown and subdued.

"Well, Don," I said, "so you want to be single again?"

"Yes I do," he said nervously, "Our kids are both at college. We're financially secure. I love Mary and will always love her but I'm fifty-two and worked hard all my life and now I want to strike out and do new things with new people and lead a more interesting and challenging life." Mary began crying again and when she stopped we all agreed on a schedule of weekly meetings. They then spontaneously spent the rest of this hour and the next several sessions telling me about the history of their relationship and their marriage.

Both came from Kansas small-town, middle-class, religious, Baptist families. They met at graduate school and married soon after graduation. They easily found teaching jobs together in Connecticut and he quickly rose to become principal. They had two children, now both away at college. They lived a quiet, orderly, congenial life, took occasional vacations to visit their families and rarely quarreled.

The therapy hours then took on a pattern of repetitious routine. They would enter my office with her looking devastated and him looking guilty and downcast. She would usually begin by reproaching him while sobbing frequently, "How can you do this to me—after so many years—what will the children say—how can you be so cruel—after all I've done for you—now you want to abandon me—etc., etc." He would then respond with unconvincing assurances, "Don't cry—I'll always love you—we'll still be friends—I'm sorry but I must be free—you'll be all right—etc., etc."

Meanwhile, I would sit there feeling like a guilty bystander, essentially ignored by both parties. Occasionally, when there was a silent interlude I would intone something like, "It's clear to me that you both care for each other very much." But this only seemed to make their anguish worse. Feeling I had to do something to break the impasse, I finally said, "Mary, it appears that when you asked Don for a trial period of marriage counseling you hoped that reproaches and appeals might persuade him to change his mind. Surely, you must be aware that this is not working." She nodded her agreement and resumed weeping. Don continued his sorrowful but stubborn determination to go forward with his plan to divorce. I decided that unless some change occurred soon I would suggest termination of the therapy.

The next day I received a phone call from Don. "Doctor, can I meet with you alone?"

"Not without Mary's consent and not without your understanding that I cannot offer you confidentiality about anything you may say to me. I suggest you tell Mary that you want to speak with me alone. If she agrees then come together at your regular time and have her wait in the waiting room until we are done and then she can join us for the rest of the hour."

At their next session Don entered alone and leaning forward he spoke in a low voice, "Doctor, you know it's possible to hear voices while in your waiting room."

"Don, that's true only when people speak very loudly in my office, not when we speak normally. Now why did you want a private meeting with me?"

"Doctor, I've decided you should know the real reason why I want a divorce from Mary. About three years ago I attended the annual meeting of the National Education Association in Miami. Mary did not go with me. She does not like travel. She does not like Florida. She does not like meetings, particularly where I have to attend sessions for principals only without her.

"Well, I met this woman there. She teaches psychology at a Miami high school; she's forty-two, divorced, no children, beautiful; and, I don't know why, but she was attracted to me and we hit it off almost immediately." Don became more and more excited as he spoke.

"It was love at first sight. She invited me to her apartment and for the first time in my marriage I was unfaithful and we began a fantastic affair. The sex was unbelievable. She was totally uninhibited and we made love almost without interruption for days on end. I've seen her twice since then, both times at annual meetings and now she wants me to move to Miami and live with her. I know you must be thinking I'm going through a mid-life crisis, but frankly, I don't care what you think, Doctor. All

I know is that I can't stop thinking about Sally, that's her name, and can hardly wait until I see her again." And then he too became tearful.

"Don, you may not care what I think but I think you are distressed now because you do care about what Mary thinks."

"Yes, I'm afraid it will break her heart."

"Don, no one dies of a broken heart. She has a right to know the truth and I'm sure she can handle it. I urge you to tell her now what you've just told me. I will bring her in and leave the two of you alone in my office for about half-an-hour. I'll be out in the waiting room and when the two of you are ready, you can call me in."

"Are you kidding? I can't do that."

"No, I'm deadly serious. You must do it. As I cautioned you, I cannot keep what you've told me secret from Mary. I am her therapist as well as yours. It is better that she hears this from you rather than from me. You and Mary must both face the truth about your situation and decide what's best for you, Mary and Sally. Don't worry, I'll be in the waiting room in case you need help."

A half hour later I re-entered my office. To my surprise Don and Mary were passionately embracing each other. Turning to me Mary explained, "Don has told me about Sally but he insists he still loves me. So I've asked him to give me some time to prove to him that I'm ready and willing to be for him whatever she is for him and maybe even more. I love him and didn't realize that all these years he was wishing I were more glamorous and sexy. I've never been aggressive with him sexually because he's never asked and I didn't think he wanted me to be that way. I don't mind being more glamorous and sexy if that will give him pleasure." Don stood by silent and beaming. We agreed to meet the following week as scheduled.

When they appeared a week later I was delighted to see their remarkable transformation. Mary was spruced up with hair attractively coiffured, full make-up, smart looking red knee-length dress, small garnet earrings and cheerful smile. In marked contrast, Ed appeared disheveled, bedraggled, rumpled and exhausted. He collapsed into his usual chair and began to shake his head and laugh.

"It's fantastic, Doctor. Mary has become a different person, full of fun and surprises. I'm having trouble keeping up with her and I'm not getting much sleep either these nights. She's a joy to be with and I could kick myself for being such a conservative stick-in-the-mud all these years and squelching her vitality with my own inhibitions."

"Better late than never."

Mary then added, "And from now on I'm going to his meetings with him to make sure no husband-stealing Bimbo carries him off."

The hour was spent in happy reminiscences of their courtship and married life. "I suggest we quit this therapy while we're ahead." I said and they agreed.

* * * * *

Marriage counseling frequently turns into divorce counseling as the couple's incompatibilities are identified and confronted. It is crucial to the outcome that the therapist be impartial and serve both parties fairly and equally. If it turns out that the therapist cannot in good conscience be this way because his allegiance for one spouse is greater than for the other, then the counseling should include two therapists, one for each spouse.

The situation usually precludes the therapist from offering a purely nondirective therapy; and a variety of exercises and interventions are available to help the couple deal with, and hopefully overcome, their difficulties.

In the case of the Statlers, the basic problem seems to have been their total lack of communication in regard to the erotic and passionate aspects of their being. This may have been the result of their fundamentalist religious indoctrination and childhood environment. The "other woman," Sally, apparently effected an awakening in the husband of his suppressed erotic self, and he, in turn, with the help of couples therapy, did the same for his wife, leading to a happy outcome and a salvaged marriage.

17

ALICE

"Doctor, may I bring a woman from my parish to see you? I'm really worried about her." This strange request came from my patient, The Reverend Albert Marsh, a young unmarried minister. He was in the process of terminating his own therapy after three months of successful treatment for his social anxiety and shyness. Shortly after graduating from divinity school he had obtained a position as minister of a small Unitarian church in a town about twenty miles from my office. As part of his ministry he offered pastoral counseling to his parishioners and Alice was one of the few who had come to him.

"She's a beautiful woman, separated from her husband, very depressed and I'm afraid she may kill herself and I don't feel I'm helping her," he pleaded. "I've tried to get her to see you but she refuses unless I go with her." I

wondered silently if my young minister patient might not
have an additional motive to want to transfer his beautiful
young patient to me . . . was he afraid he might become too
attracted to her himself?

"You know, Albert," I responded, "you seem to emphasize her beauty as if that either has something to do with
her crisis or, possibly, something to do with your eager-
ness to transfer her to me rather than treat her yourself."

"That's absurd, Doctor," he broke out. "Look, she's
really depressed about her marriage and keeps talking
about suicide. I've even urged her to go into a hospital but
she refuses. Please see her."

I agreed and the following week Reverend Marsh
appeared with Alice. She was thirty-one years old, about
five-and-a-half feet tall, slim, dark long hair, beautiful
features accented by stark make-up and wearing a simple
blue sheath dress. She sat down next to Marsh, eyes
downcast, looking quite distraught. Again I wondered
silently if my young minister patient was not more intimi-
dated by his patient's beauty than by the challenge of
treating her alleged suicidal depression. "Reverend
Marsh tells me he's worried about you," I said, "and fears
you might even commit suicide. He's asked me to see if I
can be of any help to you with your obvious distress."

Alice looked up and stared me full in the face and
spoke in a firm determined voice, "It's true that I have
wished for death, Doctor, but I have a seven-year-old
daughter who needs me and I would not want to harm her
by doing away with myself."

"I believe you," I said and after some discussion about
the possibility of psychotherapy helping her with her
marital problems and depression, she agreed to therapy
with me twice a week much to the relief of Reverend

Marsh. She kept her appointments promptly and spontaneously presented a history of her troubled life. She was
the only child of Catholic parents living in New York City.
Her father was a wealthy retired stock broker; her
mother, a housewife active in her church.

Both parents were alcoholics and quarreled inces-
santly and, on occasion, violently throughout Alice's
childhood. Sometimes in drunken rages they would beat
Alice, and she lived in constant fear of their physical
abuse. She did poorly in private school and as an adolescent became part of a wild, undisciplined group of teenagers who indulged in alcohol, marihuana, crack cocaine,
promiscuous sex, vandalism and petty crime.

Her behavior shocked her parents into resolving to
reform themselves and with the help of Alcoholics Anonymous plus pastoral counseling from their priest they
became teetotalers. But their efforts to reform Alice also
proved futile and their harangues and reproaches only
further aggravated their stormy relationship with her.

At age sixteen Alice became pregnant without knowing which of her drunken compatriots was the father. Her
parents vetoed her wish to have an abortion and she
dropped out of school and finally gave birth to a baby
daughter. Her mother took care of the baby while Alice
went to secretarial school and eventually found employment at a university hospital in New York. She continued
to drink excessively and date disreputable men, much to
the disgust of her parents, but she was able to maintain
sobriety at her secretarial job and was highly regarded
and well liked by the doctors who worked and did their
research there.

Finally, Doctor Clarence Reed, a young physician on a
fellowship in cardiology at the hospital, approached her

for a date and soon began courting her seriously. "He was the first guy I ever dated who didn't try to get me into bed," she said ironically, "and when I invited him to get sexual, he told me he was Catholic and a virgin and wanted to wait till we were married before we had sex. I told him about my daughter and he promised to adopt and care for her."

Her parents were overjoyed at the courtship and sponsored a lavish wedding. However, to Alice's dismay her husband showed little interest in sex with her, starting with their honeymoon. When confronted he claimed that her excessive drinking and alcoholic breath prevented him from having sexual feelings for her. However, even when she abstained from alcohol he still took no initiative and would submit only passively to her advances. She soon resumed her heavy drinking and their marriage rapidly deteriorated to a celibate relationship with frequent quarreling almost identical to the stormy marriage of Alice's parents during her childhood. When he accepted a staff position at a Connecticut hospital they moved nearby and, finally, she sought help from Reverend Marsh.

"You've made it clear that you are very unhappy with your marriage but, somehow, never say why you stay married to him."

"Well, for one, he has a good relationship with my daughter who loves him very much; and, for two, I have no source of income other than his salary; and, for three, my parents dote on him and would never forgive me if I should split with him."

Paradoxically, one week after this exchange, Alice came to her hour exuberant. "I did what you said and threw him out and I feel great!" I felt shocked to learn that

Alice had inferred from my comment about her not saying why she stayed in such an unhappy marriage, that I was indirectly telling her to end the marriage!

"Alice, I'm afraid you've used my remark as a way of avoiding feeling responsible for your own decision to end your marriage. But what happened to your points one, two and three?"

Alice had no answer and was chagrined at having to face the consequences of her impulsive action. Her husband began legal proceedings to obtain custody of her daughter whom he had adopted after their marriage. As Alice had predicted, her parents were furious over her action, aligned themselves with her husband and informed her they did not want to see her again. Worst of all, Alice's daughter became very upset over the absence of her father, particularly since he refused to see his daughter after Alice refused to allow him to have unsupervised visitation because of her fear that he would not return her daughter to her. Also, he refused to pay for her therapy.

Both her husband and her parents refused to send her any funds pending her husband's custody lawsuit. Alice employed a lawyer but was shaken by the array of hostile recriminations coming from husband, parents and daughter. Her despair increased and she persuaded me to prescribe an antidepressant, also a sedative for her insomnia and a tranquilizer for her anxiety.

We continued to meet twice a week even though she warned me that her husband would no longer pay for her therapy and her health insurance did not cover extended psychotherapy. Two weekends later I received an urgent phone call. It was Alice. "Doctor Fierman, I've just swallowed all the pills you prescribed for me and I'm feeling faint and dizzy. Will you come over right away!"

Her speech was slurred and I became fearful for her life and decided not to try and reason with the emergency over the phone. "Alice!" I said. "I want you to drink some hot coffee and take a cold shower!" Hoping to reassure her I decided to add, "And don't worry, I'll be right over," even though I had no intention of doing so, particularly since she lived over twenty miles away. Instead I phoned the police in her town, told them about the crisis and they agreed to go immediately to her home and take her to the emergency room of a nearby hospital. They would ask a neighbor to look after her child.

I phoned the hospital emergency room and alerted the physician in charge about her impending arrival. "What do you want me to do with her?" he asked. "Doctor," I responded, "she will be *your* patient while she's there and you must use your own clinical judgement in dealing with her. I intend to continue to be available to her as her psychotherapist and I don't wish to be involved in whatever decision you make about her management in view of her suicidal behavior." He agreed.

Hours later he phoned to inform me that he had gavaged her stomach, assessed her as being suicidally depressed and then committed her against her will to a nearby psychiatric hospital. He added that she was furious with me for calling the police and also for my not coming to the hospital emergency room to direct her treatment there.

Two days later, to my dismay I received a phone call from Alice. She bitterly informed me that she was home again, having been discharged from the psychiatric hospital against medical advice. Apparently, she had phoned another psychiatrist who had agreed to come to the hospital and sign her out, claiming he was opposed to involuntary hospitalizations of suicidal patients because: "They can just as well kill themselves inside the hospital if they 'really' want to do it, so why keep them there against their will!"

Alice went on to castigate me on the phone and announced she had arranged to go to this other psychiatrist for therapy and would never see me again. About a month later she phoned, apologized for her behavior, claimed she now accepted my rationale for my duplicitous behavior during her crisis, announced she had left her other psychiatrist whom she regarded as a fool, and requested that I resume her therapy with her. I agreed.

The therapy continued with Alice giving up her excessive drinking and showing increasing maturity and independence in her overall behavior. Then a setback occurred when her parents called to ask that Alice's daughter come to spend the Easter weekend holiday with them in New York. When Alice responded by saying she and her daughter would be happy to visit them for Easter, they corrected her, saying, "You don't understand—we don't want to see you; we only want our granddaughter to be with us!"

Alice relapsed into depression and her constant weeping during her hours alarmed me. I worried about a recurrence of her suicidal behavior and urged a period of brief hospitalization but she refused, warning, "Don't try any of your hospitalization stunts with me again. You know I'll just get someone to sign me out again if you do."

I then urged that we increase our meetings to three times a week instead of two. She declined saying that she was already distressed that her husband was not paying any of my bills ever since they had separated months before and she didn't want to increase her debt. "Don't worry," she said, drying her tears, "I'll see you next week."

Next week never came for her. She hung herself two days later.

*   *   *   *   *

The suicide of a patient while receiving psychotherapy is the most dreaded nightmare for all psychotherapists, comparable to a surgeon having his patient die while on the operating table. However, as with all failed therapies, the suicide of a patient challenges the therapist to review and reflect on where and how he erred in his judgment and behavior, and what he would do differently if he had the chance, or if similar circumstances ever occurred with future patients.

With Alice, my reflection and review led me to wish I had hospitalized her, even against her will, when I felt concerned about her suicidal potential, particularly in view of her past impulsive suicidal behavior. The law gives that power to a physician and it should be exercised when indicated, even though the therapy relationship may be terminated by the angry patient.

Also, in regard to my futile effort to increase the frequency of her therapy hours, I wish I had persisted more and not accepted her refusal based on her concern that her husband would not pay her therapy bills. Once a commitment to a therapy has been made by a therapist, he should avoid as much as possible compromising the therapy because of financial reasons. It is ironic with Alice, that soon after her death, her husband mailed a check to pay in full for her therapy.

Finally, I wish I had communicated more openly with Alice my concerns about her suicidal potential. Her situation was formidable. Her parents, husband and child were all hostile to her. She had no support system other

than her psychotherapist. Even her minister seemed to
have abandoned her. While sometimes, just that single
therapeutic relationship may be enough for an individual
to cherish life more than death, for Alice it was not.

18

FACING
PARANOID RAGE

Marjorie Rawlings, M.S.W., was a licensed social worker who was Director of a local Family Service Agency. She was self-referred, having heard about me from one of her case workers, a former patient of mine. She was forty-nine, about six feet tall, quite muscular, wearing brown tweed jacket and skirt, low-heeled shoes, thick-lensed glasses, frizzy brown hair, no make-up and a fixed, grim, frowning expression. She plunked down on the recliner facing mine and began:

"I'll come right to the point, Dr. Fierman. I'm troubled from time to time by intrusive thoughts and it seems to be getting worse. No one knows it around here but I was hospitalized when I was twenty, diagnosed schizophrenic and had shock treatments. And every few months the thoughts come back, telling me to kill myself. Usually they go away after a few weeks, but this time it's been over a month and getting worse and I'm afraid . . . I'm afraid I'm going psychotic again!" Her voice got shrill and loud and she appeared increasingly agitated.

I thought I'd better try to calm her down and head off a possible panic attack. My usual strategy in such a situation was to make a lengthy and rambling statement, which in the past had been effective in "talking down" agitated patients. I began: "I think it was wise of you to decide to get some help with your symptoms now before things got worse. Fortunately, there are medications that are helpful and also psychotherapy can be very useful. I'd like to hear your ideas as to the meaning of your intrusive thoughts and why they tell you to suicide. I'm sure you must have some notion about it. People who have such thoughts usually . . ." on and on I droned.

"I won't take any of your dreadful medications," she interrupted, "and I know damned well what those thoughts mean. Those thoughts are the voice of my grand-father who drowned himself while I just stood by watch-ing him and did nothing to stop him or save him. I just stood there and watched him walk right into the lake until the water was over his head and he didn't come up until he was drowned and dead!" She glared at me furiously.

"That must have been an awful experience for you. When did this happen and how old were you then?"

"I was sixteen and I hated him because he and his two sons, my father and my uncle, were always raping me whenever my mother wasn't around, and I hated him and I was glad to see him drown. They would hold me down and each rape me, my own father and his lousy brother and then my grandfather too."

"Where was your mother and did you tell her?"

"She was frequently off somewhere, cleaning people's houses and when she was home, she was drunk most of the time. I tried telling her but she would just smack me and tell me to stop making up stories about them."

"And your teachers at school?"

"They were useless and stupid to boot. I just put up with it and when grandpa finally killed himself, the others stopped bothering me."

After more discussion about her abused childhood we made arrangements to meet weekly for psychotherapy. As she was leaving at the end of the session I said, "I'm glad you've come to me for therapy, Marjorie; may I call you Marjorie?" and held out my hand, thinking that would be a reassuring gesture for her, but I was wrong and it turned out to be a mistake. She appeared startled, stepped back and away from my outstretched hand, and after looking at me suspiciously, turned and silently hurried out.

The following week she strode into the office, glared at me and launched into a wild tirade: "You bastard! I know what you were up to with your filthy handshake . . . just like my grandfather . . . he would hold my hand as if he liked me and then start grabbing at me . . . you lousy men are all alike . . . always trying to stick your dirty prick into some innocent girl . . . I'm going to tear your penis out by the roots. . . ."

I was just a young full-time Yale faculty assistant professor then, moonlighting evenings to supplement my meager salary. I had rented a colleague's office for a dollar an hour and had a small caseload of psychotherapy patients. As Marjorie escalated her furious recriminations and threats, I became anxiously aware that she was my last patient of the evening, that we two were the only ones in the building at that late hour, that she was seated between me and the office door so no easy flight was available, and, finally, that she was larger, taller and more muscular than I and appeared quite capable and increasingly motivated to engage me in a violent battle. Furthermore, she appeared to be quite psychotic and paranoid.

I sat there frozen with fear, stiff and motionless, wide-eyed and silent as she ranted: "I'm going to kill you, you son-of-a-bitch . . . I come here for help and all you can think of is getting into my pants . . . you ought to be ashamed and you're not going to get away with it . . . you're worse than my father . . . he was a stupid, uneducated, alcoholic farmer with a wife who despised him and a daughter he didn't want . . . but you're a doctor . . . a psychiatrist yet . . . and all you care about is seducing your patients . . . you deserve to die, you creep!"

As time went on she gradually began to soften her castigation of me. Her shouting lessened and, finally, she became silent, still staring at me, but now with a quizzical expression. Then, to my relief, she broke out with a broad smile: "I must say, you are one of the bravest persons I've ever met. Here I am threatening to kill you and you don't even blink an eye or say a word."

I decided not to correct her misinterpretation of my frozen terror as being bravery, and instead commented: "Marjorie, if you want me to pay full attention to whatever you have to say to me, you should not, by your threats, distract me into having to plan how to defend myself against a possible assault. But I certainly can appreciate how your being exposed to brutal incest through much of your childhood would make you suspicious of men's intentions."

Still smiling she said, "Well, it seems this therapy is working. Instead of thoughts that keep telling me to kill myself, now they just keep telling me to kill you instead."

"That does sound like improvement. My only regret is that 'I have but one life to lose for my—patients.'" We both laughed as the session ended.

Her therapy continued for several weeks without recurrence of her bizarre verbal attack. Instead she dwelt on her fearful childhood, her alcoholic parents, her depraved grandfather and uncle. But gradually her recriminations turned into sorrowful remembrances. She began to look at the pathological behavior of her own family with the same clinical perspective that characterized her approach to the patients and clients who came for help to her agency. She became less judgmental and more forgiving.

Finally, she appeared one day to report that she had been offered a new position at an out-of-state agency with better salary, staff and budget. She had decided to terminate her therapy with me and take the job. "The thoughts have gone away for now," she said, "and there's no reason we shouldn't credit your therapy. Of course, they've gone away in the past only to return later on, particularly when I've experienced increased stress. This time I can think of no new stress in my life other than going into menopause. I guess that might have caused it. You've wondered about my being single and lonely, but I have my dogs and my gardening and my work. I'm usually a happy person except when my bad memories and suicidal thoughts recur. But thanks anyway for all your help."

She stood and offered me her hand. I gulped and cautiously accepted her handshake. We both laughed as she left.

* * * * *

A safe dictum for all psychotherapists is: "Look, Listen, But Don't Touch." There are better and safer ways to communicate caring, concern and support, particularly with new patients whose unique history and idiosyncracies have yet to be disclosed.

The potential for erotization of the relationship between therapist and patient is considerable in view of the "unconditional positive regard" (Rogers, 1980) offered by the therapist in his role as a confidant, and the private, isolated structure of the therapist's office. A few therapists may advocate physical contact, even a sexual relationship; but the consensus among psychotherapists is that physical relationships between therapist and patient harm the patient more than they help. They compromise the effectiveness of the therapy and leave the therapist open to charges of grave unethical and illegal conduct. With this patient even an ordinary casual handshake was misinterpreted as sexually provocative and highlights the importance of avoiding all physical contact.

This patient's horrendous childhood left her with a precariously concealed paranoid rage that periodically broke through her "mask of sanity." The therapy helped her reframe her perspective of the pathological behavior of her father, grandfather and uncle and to see them more as pathetic, deranged and morally bankrupt men rather than as evil, heartless predators. Unfortunately, she left her therapy improved but still vulnerable to relapse.

19

IF IT AIN'T BROKE
DON'T FIX IT

Doctor Bernard Baldwin was a closet transvestite—a cross-dresser. He had kept his fetishistic behavior secret from others well into his thirties when a fatal error in timing led to his exposure. His wife, Edna, had gone off for her weekly evening of bridge with friends, leaving him at home to baby-sit with their four-year-old daughter and two-year-old son. As soon as they were asleep, he was into his wife's bureau, feverishly donning her bra, pantyhose, dress, slippers and long-haired blond party wig. He was just preparing to apply her mascara and make-up when in she walked since her bridge game had been canceled.

"Berny!" she screamed, "what are you doing!" and began to weep since the answer to her question was apparent in the form of her husband's female transformation.

"It was awful, Doctor Fierman," Bernard said in my office after describing the above scenario. "Edna kept crying and berating me, calling me a faggot, threatening divorce and even ordering me out of our house. I finally calmed her down by promising I would go into therapy with you and wouldn't wear women's clothes any more. But I'm not sure I can keep that promise."

"Perhaps you are not sure you really want to give up cross-dressing."

"Not so. I really do want to stop. But you must know how it is; whenever I feel tense or frustrated or angry or upset in any way, I have this urge to dress up and, if the circumstances permit, I'll masturbate. It relieves me; it's like I'm back with my mother—being in women's clothes is like being inside her—she was a saint and loved me unconditionally—I was an only child and only thirteen when my father was killed in a plane crash—he was a corporate lawyer and flew around the country in chartered planes to see his clients—there were other lawyers on the plane who survived the crash and heard my dad call out to them that he was dying and ask them to tell my mother and me that he loved us."

Doctor Baldwin choked up and cried during this account of his father's death and then continued: "As a young kid I sometimes played with my parents' shoes or clothes, but after my dad's death I found that I could find peace and calm and comfort by wearing my mother's clothes and masturbating. I would fantasy that I was a woman having sex with a lesbian. But don't get me wrong; I'm no homosexual—I love women and have no sexual urges for men. But when I have sex with a woman I usually have that same fantasy: I'm a woman having sex with a lesbian.

"You know, Doctor Fierman, I feel very good telling you all this stuff. You're the first person I've ever told my secrets to and it's a great relief."

Doctor Baldwin was thirty-four, six feet tall, slim, trim and athletic, brunette wavy hair, ruddy complexion, rimless glasses, starched white shirt and dark bow-tie; smiling and beaming at me with no trace of shame or distress about being a cross-dresser. He had informed me that he was an internist and an assistant clinical professor at Yale Medical School. His wife, Edna, a classmate at college, was an artist and a volunteer at the university hospital. He claimed they were a happy couple until his wife discovered his cross-dressing.

"She's moved into our guest bedroom and hardly talks to me. She accuses me of betraying her by having this secret problem. I've asked her to see a therapist with me, but she refuses; claims it's my problem and that I have to change or else she's going to divorce me."

"You sound as if you agree with her."

"I do agree with her. It's crazy and stupid behavior and if I were ever caught it would scandalize my family and my career. She would have every right to divorce me if you don't cure me of this compulsion."

This became the theme of Bernard's weekly psycho-therapy sessions over the next several weeks. He would report his wife's unrelenting castigating of his secret cross-dressing; then he would defend her behavior as being justified in view of his heinous disorder. My attempts to soften his self-condemnation were rejected. Finally he began complaining that the therapy was not lessening his increasing desire to cross-dress again.

"Bernard," I had occasion to say, "it seems you are angry with me because you feel I don't treat your alleged compulsion with more respect."

"Damn right!" he broke out, "You treat it like a joke even though it's ruining my marriage and threatening my career."

"But look at the facts, Bernard. You are hurting no one. You are discreet. You have found a way to comfort yourself in times of stress. It's your own self-flagellation and efforts to deny your own desire to cross-dress that keeps your fantasies and urges alive and intense. I suspect that if you were more accepting of your own innocent idiosyncracies, they might well disappear over time. Think of all the people who cross-dress without any distress about it."

"Like who?" he said angrily.

"Well, let's start with the Romans of history in their togas; then go to the priests through the ages and up to the present; the Scots in their kilts; the Mandarins of the Orient; the Shakespearean male actors who portrayed women in his plays; the famous basketball player, Dennis Rodmam, and in New York, Mayor Giuliani."

Somehow, my diatribe seemed to break through his glum distress and he began to laugh. I then invited him to join an ongoing weekly group therapy that I and my psychologist wife had formed consisting of patients of ours and also patients of other colleagues who shared our offices. He agreed and in the meetings he shared his dilemma about cross-dressing and received sympathetic support from both the men and the women in the group.

A few weeks later the group therapy session began at its scheduled time in my office as group members were straggling in. A few minutes later there was a knock at the door. I stood up and went to the door, opened it and was surprised to see a blond, statuesque, shapely woman standing there in a striking sequined yellow evening gown. She wore modest but attractive jewelry and make-up. "Dr. Fierman?" she asked sweetly.

"Yes?" I answered awkwardly.

"May I come in and join your group?"

After staring at her for several seconds I suddenly realized who it was. "Dr. Baldwin!" I exclaimed and with manicky excitement the four other men in the group joined me at the doorway to greet our transvestite group member, applauding, shaking his hand, and hugging him enthusiastically. After he took his seat and the celebration calmed down it was apparent that the four women in the group had not joined in the hilarity but instead had remained seated, bewildered and silently staring at this strange intruder into their feminine domain.

The group therapy session continued with the men eagerly engaging Bernard in lively conversation, inquiring and admiring his garb and artistry in portraying a voluptuous and seductive female. The women, at first cool and distant, gradually became more friendly and accepting with occasional quizzical comments and some expressions of ridicule directed toward the men in the group for their gleeful reaction to Bernard's cross-dressing.

Bernard never repeated his cross-dressed appearance at group sessions or in his individual hours with me, but it was clear there had been a turning point. He clearly no longer agreed with his wife's condemnation of his cross-dressing. He purchased his own supply of female clothes, lingerie, costume jewelry and make-up and on occasions when he was alone at home, or alone in his study even while his wife was home, he would don his female clothes and relax with fantasies about lesbian sex.

He reported that at some risk he had stood up to his wife and defended his cross-dressing and that she finally was persuaded that it need not be a deterrent to their continued happy marital and sexual relationship. Still undecided, however, was how he would deal with his children if and when they became aware of his cross-dressing. He decided to put that issue off until they were older but conceded that he might renounce his cross-dressing completely if his relationship with his children was threatened by it.

"So long, Doctor Fierman," he said warmly at the close of his last hour with me, shaking my hand vigorously, "I'll be calling you again, if my 'hobby' ever gets me in trouble again."

So far he has not called.

*   *   *   *   *

Not all deviant behavior is sufficiently aberrant or disaster-threatening to warrant ruthless eradication. This patient's sense of inner well-being was maintained by a relatively harmless personal and private behavior, albeit psychopathological. The nonjudgmental attitude of his therapist and his group therapy colleagues supported his self-esteem in spite of his deviant behavior and permitted him to continue a satisfying life without making major changes in his own behavior patterns.

This patient had a mild form of "Transvestic Fetishism." It did not interfere seriously with his personal, marital or professional life and he was not seriously motivated to use psychotherapy to free himself from his private compulsion. Instead, his therapy freed him from his self-condemnation, restored his self-esteem and encouraged him to establish a more open and intimate relationship with his wife.

20

AN EXORCISM

"Doctor Fierman, I don't really know why I'm here or what I want you to do for me—people told me you were a good therapist and—and," she broke down crying with sobbing gasps and choked-off moans, rocking back and forth, dabbing at tears with her handkerchief. I handed her a box of tissues. After several minutes I tried to console her. "Doctor Rogers, you sound as if you feel you have to justify your coming here. . . . Your tears are justification enough."

She gradually calmed down, sat up primly, took a deep breath and began haltingly: "Edward—my husband—is ill—seriously ill—and he blames me. Maybe he's right. Maybe I have caused his illness, but I do love him even though I'm getting a divorce."

She went on to explain that she had married Edward while they were in college together. She had gone on to medical school while he entered a master's program in business administration. She was now a medical intern in a local hospital while he worked for a local manufacturing company. A year ago she discovered he was having an affair with a friend of theirs. She became very upset and asked for a divorce even though he pledged future fidelity. She refused to reconsider and while she proceeded with arrangements for a divorce he began to develop back pains.

Jane Rogers wept again as she spoke about her husband's suffering. He had developed recurrent sharp pains in his lower back for several months now. The pains would strike suddenly and he would scream and fall down and writhe in agony for several minutes until the pains would gradually subside. He then would be well for a few days until another attack occurred. Their local physician could find no organic cause of the attacks. He then diagnosed Edward as having a "Hysterical Conversion Reaction" secondary to the stress of the impending divorce and referred him to a psychiatrist. She then decided to get help for her own troubled state and was referred to me.

We agreed to meet weekly and after several sessions it became clear that she was dubious about her husband's diagnosis. "Jane," I said, "you've indicated in several ways that you disagree with Edward's doctor and that you do not think he has a conversion hysteria, yet you resist seeking another medical opinion."

"I do have my doubts, Doctor Fierman, but as I've told you, Ed refuses to go to another doctor, and besides, our insurance will not pay for it."

I stifled my inner feelings of dismay over her passivity and stared silently at my weeping patient. She was short, trim, pretty, well dressed and clearly smart and competent, but she did have a history of being passive in her relationship with her father, older brothers and authority figures in general. For her to challenge both her husband and his doctor would be difficult but not impossible, and that was where my attention became focused in her therapy.

"Jane," I said at the opening of her next session, "it seems you have a dilemma as to whether to keep silent and avoid challenging Ed's doctor or whether to insist that Ed get another opinion even if your insurance will not pay for it."

"You really want me to do that, don't you?"

After a few minutes of reflection on what she had just said, I answered, "It seems you would prefer to resolve your dilemma by invoking my opinion rather than by deciding for yourself?"

She glared at me silently, exasperated and obviously annoyed.

After several minutes I decided to break the silence and said, "You look as if you think I should be shot at sunrise for cruelty to patients."

She laughed and explained, "No, it's only that I'm embarrassed by my reluctance to act assertively. My father was a surgeon and dominated the family. He insisted that I go into medicine, and I'm glad I did, but I do feel anxious whenever I have to deal with superiors, particularly men. But you're right. I'm reasonably sure that Ed has some kind of medical or orthopedic problem with his back and I am going to insist we get a consultation."

My pleasure over what appeared to be progress in her therapy was dashed a week later when she appeared tearful and distraught. She reported that her husband had finally consulted another orthopedist who did a more thorough work-up and discovered that Ed, a cigarette smoker, had lung cancer with metastasis to his spine. His prognosis for life beyond a year or so was grim.

For the following year the therapy for my grieving patient consisted mainly of trying to console and support her. She elected to indulge her husband throughout his extended chemotherapy and radiation although she knew he was continuing his extramarital relationship. They finally agreed to a friendly divorce, and when his condition became terminal he entered Hospice and finally died with both women at his bedside.

To my dismay a few weeks after his death she reported anxiously in her therapy that she had developed recurrent pains in her back similar to that which her husband had endured! She also reported that she was being courted by a fellow intern and they were seriously considering becoming committed to each other. "Doctor Fierman," she exclaimed, "the pains started once Mike and I became serious about our relationship. I know it sounds crazy but I keep thinking that somehow, Ed is doing this to me!"

She became silent, staring at me expectantly.

"Jane, it sounds as if there's a point you want to make but are having some sort of difficulty saying it."

"Yes there is. Don't you see?" she cried out, "I need an exorcism! Ed is doing this to me because he doesn't want me to marry Mike!"

I felt completely nonplussed. The troubling thought occurred to me that my patient might be slipping into some sort of psychotic break. I knew that she was a non-practicing Catholic and was still severely distressed by her ex-husband's infidelity, painful illness and death, but I also knew she was an intelligent, sophisticated physician. It seemed incongruous that she should be seriously talking about demonic possession and considering an exorcism for her back pains.

I had never dealt before with a case of alleged "possession," but was familiar with both the movie, *The Exorcist*, and Paddy Chayefsky's play, *The Tenth Man*, that also portrayed an exorcism.

In the next few sessions she revealed that in her childhood she had received intensive Catholic schooling by nuns and priests and had been devout throughout her early life with her family. But when she left her family to go to college and medical school, her faith rapidly dwindled and she finally discontinued all formal religious practice.

"Well, Jane," I said, "if you seriously think exorcism will help you, why don't you arrange to have a priest do it?"

"No," she said emphatically, "I don't want a priest. I want you to do it!"

I told her I would need some time to consider her request and received her permission to consult with an elderly friend of mine who was both a retired clinical psychologist and also an ordained rabbi. I arranged to meet with Doctor Jacob Bergman for lunch.

Now in his 80s, Doctor Bergman was tall, gaunt and physically frail, but still alert and intense. The hair on his head had thinned out, but his long gray beard and piercing eyes gave him a patriarchal appearance consistent with his reputation as a wise and skillful psychotherapist. We had been friends for many years. He listened carefully to my story about Jane.

"Jake," I concluded, "my patient is very distraught and still in mourning over the death of her ex-husband and I hate to turn her down or confront her with the weirdness of her wanting to be exorcised."

"Let's face it, Lou," Doctor Bergman finally commented, "for many people psychiatry has replaced religion. Your patient has placed in you the faith she used to

have in priests. You can either attempt in your psychotherapy sessions to work through her dependent fixation
on you and her obsession with exorcism or, if you feel her
situation is more urgent, you can indulge her now and try
to relieve her of her hysterical back pains by doing an
exorcism. It's your choice!"

For a week I obsessed about my dilemma. Jane's pains
had become more intense and frequent and she had been
cleared by her own doctors of having any organic pathology that might account for her pains. She obviously now
met the criteria for a diagnosis of conversion hysteria. But
was it ethical for me, a psychiatrist, to grant her request
and perform an exorcism? Or was it ethical for me to
allow her agony to continue while I tried to relieve her
crisis with psychotherapy?

My dilemma was finally resolved when I reasoned that
effective psychotherapy could be seen, in a way, as a form
of slow exorcism. A psychotherapist cures his patients by
offering a healing relationship that gradually frees the
patient of all the devils and demons of his past that have
possessed his autonomy, creativity and independence.

Now it was my patient, Jane, who was in the grasp of
a delusion that the spirit of her dead ex-husband had taken
possession of her body to torment her and prevent her
from finding happiness and love with another man. But
she also seemed willing and able to give up her guilt-
ridden fantasy if only I, a healer and therapist, to whom
she had transferred her childhood religious faith and
trust, would perform an ancient and magical ritual. Why
shouldn't I comply and make the attempt to grant her
desperate request?

Of course, I was concerned that performing an exorcism was inconsistent with providing effective psychotherapy in that it certainly would not be maturizing and

also would reinforce and promote magical thinking. But this concern was overcome by my greater fear that my patient seemed to be on the brink of a worsening serious delusional paranoid state of mind. I decided that under these unusual circumstances, it would be an appropriate crisis intervention.

We arranged to meet in my office in the evening. As luck would have it, there was a full moon that night. As I had directed, she brought a picture of Ed, his wedding ring, his tennis racket, a pair of his gloves and his old sneakers. I lit a large candle and some incense and turned off the lights. Jane reclined on the office couch while I placed all the articles of Ed that she had brought on the floor next to the couch and then sat on a chair facing her.

We remained silent, breathing the incense-laden air and looking at each other in the flickering candlelight and moonlight shining through the window. Jane began to sob softly. My own breathing became labored and I began to feel oppressed. In the dim light Ed's sneakers and racket seemed to pulsate. I began to perspire and my heart began to beat rapidly as I fantasized his presence in the room.

"Edward Rogers!" I called out loudly, "I demand that you leave Jane's body now and forever! You've had your life with her and now you must let her have her life without you. She still loves you and will love you for the rest of her life, but you must leave her now and never again interfere with her new relationships and her new loves. Go in peace and leave Jane in peace!"

I was trembling and amazed at my own spontaneous and unprepared pronouncements. Jane was sitting up, staring wide-eyed at me, looking also amazed at the fervor of my exhortations.

After a long silence I finally blew out the candle and turned on the office lights. "Jane," I said, "Ed is now gone and will not trouble you again and your pains will also not trouble you anymore. I want you to take his things and bury them in your back yard and say good-bye to Ed once and for always. I'll see you at our regular time next week."

Jane arrived at her following session smiling and cheery. "I feel fine. The pains are gone, thanks to you," she said. The next few sessions dealt with her growing romance with Mike. She terminated her therapy shortly afterwards. Later she married Mike and continued with her medical career, apparently without recurrence of neurotic symptoms.

* * * * *

I had grave doubts about including this story about an exorcism in an anthology of stories about the therapy of patients of mine. While I was confident that my decision to agree to my patient's request that I perform an exorcism was an appropriate creative crisis intervention, I was concerned that readers would regard it as an ill-conceived counter-transference maneuver. Should I publish such a controversial therapy or not? I decided to seek consultation.

My psychologist wife thought publication might harm my reputation and advised against it. A psychologist friend also advised against publication because of his concern that it would encourage unskilled therapists to engage in inappropriate or even unethical activities in their therapies. However, a psychiatrist friend advised that I include the story in order to stimulate other therapists to be more creative in their therapies and to focus more on the problems that patients present and how to best solve them. His advice prevailed and with some trepidation I decided to include the story. Psychotherapies sometimes require an "experiment" to break through the resistance and rigidity of neurotic, defensive psychopathology. If the therapist can comfortably and temporarily put aside his usual rational perspectives and patterns of interaction with patients and allow his own fantasies to participate, he may successfully overcome an impasse or crisis in a particular therapy. Of course, there is the risk of failure and possibly aggravating the problem, but there is also the chance of effecting a happy outcome.

The psychoanalytic concept of "regression in the service of the ego" is relevant here. Creativity and inspiration in the arts has been viewed by analysts as involving the temporary opening of the artist's mind to primitive and alogical thought processes and applying those images to the artistic work. So it can be in psychotherapy when under special circumstances the therapist and the patient both put aside their objectivity and join in an experimental fantasy, invoking magical and supernatural forces in order to overcome an impasse or crisis in the therapy. As with hypnosis, the power of suggestion may be effective in persuading a patient to relinquish an unhealthy belief system.

In regard to her husband's death from metastatic cancer after his previous physician had diagnosed "conversion hysteria," clinicians should always keep in mind that when somatic complaints are given such a diagnosis, it may in fact only indicate that the patient's physician had been unable to establish any medical/organic diagnosis rather than that there were positive signs and symptoms of a psychological illness.

21

THE SHY BACHELOR

"I'm taking this course in pastoral counseling at the Divinity School, Doctor, and we were supposed to bring a dream to class and I volunteered my dream for discussion. Well, the dream was that I was wandering about in this old country house that my folks had in Maine, where we used to spend summers, and all the furniture was covered with white sheets . . . and I kept looking for my parents and my brother and sister, but all was quiet and I went up the stairs to the bedrooms and when I came to my parents' room, the door was shut . . . and I opened the door slowly and there was my mother sitting up in her bed in her nightgown with her hair all gray and down to her shoulders and I could see by the way she was staring past me that she was blind! And then I woke up.

"Well, the teacher said he did not think that was a dream to discuss in the class and advised that I see him privately in his office afterwards. When I did meet with him, he said he thought the dream meant that I harbored a death wish toward my mother. That shook me up terribly and I began crying so he then advised that I get some therapy and recommended you."

Charles Davis was stretched out on the couch to which he had gone directly on entering my office. He was twenty-two, tall, athletic build, ruddy complexion, dressed casually, articulate and intelligent. He seemed puzzled that he could still see me seated near the couch, and shifted his body so that he could no longer see me. "Aren't you supposed to be sitting behind the couch so that your patients don't see you?"

"No."

"Well, what do you think of my dream?"

"I would think that if you truly wished your mother were dead, you would know it without having to learn about it in a dream."

"'Wish my mother were dead!' What are you saying? I love my mother. She's my best friend. I would die for her! I would never have such a wish. That's ridiculous! . . . But then what does my dream mean?"

"You've just made the point that the last person you consulted gave you an interpretation that you regard as ridiculous, and now you want another person to give you another interpretation. I would think you would go to the author of your dream to explain it to you."

"Author? You mean me? I haven't a clue."

"Neither do I."

"Well, maybe if you knew more about me you would be more able to help me understand it."

"You've come for therapy to help you understand your dreams?"

"Well, there's more than that. I've been shy and nervous all my life but it's gotten worse lately, particularly around girls and superiors and senior professionals. I rarely date because I'm afraid of being turned down, and even more afraid of not being turned down. Maybe if I told you about my life history, you'd understand my problems better. Isn't that what I'm supposed to do here, anyway?"

"No."

"Well, what am I supposed to do here? How am I supposed to begin?"

"You've already begun. And while it's not that you are supposed to do nothing here, there is nothing you are supposed to do here. You are free to do whatever you wish, within reason and common sense, you understand."

"Well," he said, becoming irritated, "is it OK with you if I tell you the story of my life?"

"You seem to have trouble believing I meant what I said."

"You said I could do whatever I wanted to do here, within reason. Right?"

"Right"

"Well, I want to tell you about my life history. OK?"

"It's OK with me."

For the rest of the hour and in the weekly sessions that followed, Charles launched into a lengthy and detailed chronological history of his life. He had been born in New York. His father had been a prominent minister but died of a heart attack at age fifty, when Charles was twelve. Charles had an older married brother, also a minister in New York, and a younger unmarried sister, a New York nurse. He did well in private schools and was now a senior at the Yale Divinity School. He had been active in sports throughout his academic years and had many friends but no serious attachments. His socializing had always been with a group of his friends, but he had not risked dating singly. He was a devout Episcopalian and was still virginal. When alone with a woman or a superior he would experience sweating and palpitations and an occasional migraine headache. His family physician had found him to be in good physical health with no medical or cardiovascular abnormalities that would account for his symptoms.

After about four weekly sessions had passed I became concerned that he clearly behaved as if he were in compliance with some unspoken directive from me calling on him to present his life history as necessary for his therapy to be effective. "Charles," I said, "although you originally said you wanted to tell me your life history so that I would understand your problems better, you sound more and more as if you think I or your therapy requires that you leave no detail out of your chronology. Also for some reason you seem to believe that the best way to talk to me about yourself is to lie on the couch, stare at the ceiling and have me listen while you present your history."

Silence. Charles appeared stunned by my statement. Then slowly he sat up and faced me, glaring angrily. "What!" he shouted, "You let me go on and on for all this time, and now you tell me that's not what you want me to do? You mean to say you don't want me to lie on the couch and report what's on my mind? Isn't that what's supposed to happen in psychoanalysis? What kind of analyst are you, any way?"

"I'm a psychotherapist," I replied, "and as I said before, you are free to do whatever you want to do here, but it is not so that I want you to lie on the couch and report your life history or the contents of your mind."

"Then why do you have this couch here, if you don't want your patients to lie on it?"

"I use it to rest on when I feel tired and also for my patients, including yourself, to use if they so desire."

"This is terrible," he said, "and it's not what I expected. . . . Do you mind if I consult with other psychiatrists in the area. I may decide to go to someone more traditional than you."

"Do you want to stop your therapy with me?" I asked.

"I'm not sure, but if you don't mind, I'd like to talk to some other therapists about the possibility of changing."

"I don't mind." I said, although I did feel uneasy about the thought of his talking to my colleagues about me.

The following week Charles appeared looking stern and frowning. "I went to see Doctor Williams and when I told him about your therapy with me he shook his head and advised me to switch. But he was booked up for about six months, so he gave me the name of Doctor Robertson and I'm going to see him next week. However, I do want to keep on with you until I decide whether or not to change, if that's OK with you. Meanwhile, are you sure you don't mind if I have interviews with other analysts in the area?"

"Well, I mind only in the sense of feeling sorry that you are dissatisfied with your therapy with me," I replied. Charles then returned to his life-history narrative. The following two weeks were replays, each time he would report on the critical statements of the analysts he was consulting, but somehow never arranging to become their patient. I silently became increasingly annoyed with the thought of his meeting with all my colleagues, but felt it would not be helpful either to him or his therapy for me to complain. I could only hope that there would be an early end to what had become an ordeal for me.

To my surprise and relief at his next session he entered with a broad smile, plunked himself down in the recliner facing me and reported, "Well, I saw Doctor Goldblatt yesterday and he told me he knew you and has heard you lecture and he thinks you're a fine therapist and saw no reason for me to stop, so I've decided to continue with you."

"Charles," I said, "I'm happy to continue your therapy and that you're through discussing me with my colleagues in this town. But I do want to share an association I have. I'm reminded of the movie, *The Wizard of Oz*; when the cowardly lion asks the Wizard for courage, the Wizard tells the lion that if he will go and rescue Judy Garland from the Wicked Witch, then the Wizard will give him courage. The same kind of offer is given to the Tin Man for a heart and the Scarecrow for a brain."

"Doctor," Charles interrupted, "I haven't the slightest idea what you're talking about. What's your point?"

"Don't you see? It was a trick, When the cowardly lion bravely rescues Judy Garland he has found his courage; and when the Tin Man has the heart to endure the dangers of the rescue, he has found his heart; and when the Scarecrow figures out how to rescue Judy Garland he has found his brain." And when you brazenly consulted four psychiatrists to complain about me you obviously overcame your shyness, to say the least. Plus no mention of palpitations, sweating or migraines. Your shyness has been replaced by 'chutzpah,' if you know what that means."

He laughed, shook his head and replied, "By God, you're right. My symptoms have gone."

As his therapy progressed, he confessed that for some time he had become attracted to a young, pretty librarian in the college library. While he had been able to engage in small talk with her and had learned that she was single and living nearby with her parents, he had not risked going further. But now, armed with his new-found courage he asked for a date and to his pleasure she accepted eagerly. It was ironic that he discovered that she also suffered from shyness and this had discouraged suitors in the past. The courtship evolved rapidly, his mother and her parents all approved and supported their relationship, and soon plans for marriage were made.

"This will be my last hour with you", he announced one day, "and I never did find out why I had so much anxiety and shyness in the first place. Does that mean I'm at risk for a relapse?"

"No. But, as you know, I'm as close to you as the telephone or your E-Mail." At the end of the session he parted with a warm handshake. Later I received news of his graduation, his subsequent marriage and the birth of their son. He had become minister of a congregation on Long Island.

About five years later I received a phone call from his wife. Charles was ill in a New Haven hospital, probably dying from metastatic melanoma and had asked to see me. I went the following weekend and found him bedridden and emaciated but still alert and articulate. "Doctor Fierman," he said, holding my hand, "you helped me find my way to a wonderful life and I wanted to thank you before I die."

"You did it yourself," I replied, concealing my heartfelt anguish on seeing his terminal condition. "Don't you remember *The Wizard of Oz* story?"

"Yes," he smiled, "but promise me one thing. I want you to study and learn about Jesus Christ and maybe come to Him for my sake if not for yours."

"I promise," I said, determined to say whatever I could to ease his agony. We spoke a bit more about his family and then, after an emotional embrace, I left. He died a few days afterwards.

*   *   *   *   *

With therapy this patient experienced relief of his social anxiety and shyness without our ever addressing his symptoms directly. As all therapists who do so-called long-term therapy observe, patients in effective psychotherapy not only experience alleviation of those symptoms that receive discussion and focus, but also experience alleviation of other symptoms that are only slightly attended to or not even mentioned at all. The notion that insight is required to become rid of symptoms without risk of relapse is one of the myths of psychotherapy that persists.

The communicative-intimacy provided by the therapist is the potent ingredient of psychotherapy and has the power to alleviate symptoms and promote independence and autonomy. When the human spirit is liberated, neurotic inhibitions and anxieties are dissipated. This patient lived a short life but died a free spirit.

REFERENCES

Buber, M. (1923). *Ich und Du*. Leipsig: Insel-Verlag. trans. by W. Kaufman. (1970). *I and Thou*. New York: Charles Scribner and Sons.

_____(1952). Preface. In Trub H.: Heilung aus der begegnung (Healing through meeting). In *Eine Auseinendersetzung mit der Psychologie C. J. Jungs*. ed. E. Michel and A. Sborowitz. Stuttgart: Ernst Klett Verlag.

_____(1960). *The Origin and Meaning of Hasidism*. Trans. and ed. with an Introduction by M. S. Friedman. New York: Horizon Books, p. 132f.

Cushman, P. (1992). Psychotherapy to 1922: A historically situated interpretation. In *History of Psychotherapy*, ed. D. K. Freedheim. Chapter 2. pp. 21-64. Washington, D. C.: American Psychological Association.

Erikson, M. H. (1967). *Advanced Technique of Hypnosis and Therapy*, ed. J. Haley. New York: Grune & Stratton.

Evans, R. I. (1975). *Carl Rogers; The Man and His Ideas.* New York: E. P. Dulton Paperback.

Frankl, V. E. (1973). The image of man in psychotherapy. Trans. W. Hallo. In *The Worlds of Existentialism: A Critical Reader*, ed. with Introduction and Conclusions, M. S. Fricdman, p. 468. Chicago: The University of Chicago Press (paperback).

Fierman, L. B., ed. (1965). *Effective Psychotherapy / The Contribution of Hellmuth Kaiser.* New York: The Free Press / Macmillan.

_____(1997). *The Therapist Is the Therapy.* Northvale, New Jersey: Jason Aronson.

Friedman, M. (1985). *The Healing Dialogue in Psychotherapy.* Northvale, New Jersey: Jason Aronson.

Fromm, E. (1962). *Beyond the Chains of Illusion: My Encounter with Marx and Freud.* New York: Simon and Schuster (Credo Series).

Kahlbaum, K. L. (1874). *Die Katatonia Oder das Spannungsirresein.* Berlin: Hirschwald.

Kaiser, H. (1955). The problem of responsibility in psychotherapy. *Psychiatry.* 18:205-211.

_____(1965a). The universal symptom of the psychoneuroses: a search for the conditions of effective psychotherapy. In *Effective Psychotherapy / The Contribution of Hellmuth Kaiser*, ed. L. B. Fierman. pp. 14-171. New York: Free Press/Macmillan.

Knight, R. P. (1946). The psychotherapy of an adolescent catatonic schizophrenic with mutism. *Psychiatry.* 9: 323-339.

Lomas, P. (1981). *The Case for a Personal Psychotherapy.* Oxford: Oxford University Press.

_____(1987). *The Limits of Interpretation / What's Wrong With Psychoanalysis.* New York: Penguin Books.

_____(1999). *Doing Good? Psychotherapy Out Of Its Depth.* Oxford: Oxford University Press.

Raskin, N. B. (1948). The development of nondirective therapy. *Journal of Consulting Psychology.* 12:92-110.

Reich, W. (1949). *Character Analysis.* p. 57. New York: Orgone Institute Press.

Rogers, C. (1980). *A Way of Being.* Boston: Houghton Mifflin. p. 129.

Yalom, I. D. (1980). *Existential Psychotherapy.* New York: Basic Books. p. 104.

INDEX

Louis B. Fierman, M.D., is a graduate of Case Western Reserve University School of Medicine. After completing a rotating internship at Cleveland Metropolitan General Hospital, he entered active duty in the Army and was assigned to Military Government in occupied Japan. Returning to civilian life in the U.S. in 1949, he entered residency training in internal medicine at Yale, switching to psychiatry with the encouragement of his psychologist wife. He was appointed Chief Resident at both the Yale Psychiatric Institute and the Yale-New Haven Hospital Psychiatric Service, has taught psychotherapy, and remains on the clinical faculty of the Yale School of Medicine. He entered psychoanalysis with Hellmuth Kaiser, a psychoanalyst who had broken with traditional and orthodox psychoanalysis to devise a new and more effective psychotherapy. After Kaiser's death, Dr. Fierman published *Effective Psychotherapy*, an anthology of Kaiser's works.

Dr. Fierman has been President of the Connecticut Psychiatric Society, Chief of the Psychiatric Service at the West Haven Veterans Administration Medical Center, Medical Director of Elmcrest Psychiatric Institute and, as Medical Director of Psychotherapy Associates, is in private practice in New Haven, Connecticut. He is a Life Fellow of the American Psychiatric Association.

Now semi-retired, Dr. Fierman has returned to his childhood interest in classical music and plays the French horn in two local symphony orchestras.